Mark's Guide

for

Central Alberta Paddlers

1997

Mark Lund

Canadian Cataloguing in Publication Data

Lund, Mark E. R. (Mark Ernest Robert), 1951 -
   Mark's guide for central Alberta paddlers

Includes bibliographical references.
ISBN 0-9682326-0-4

   1. Canoes and canoeing - Alberta - Guidebook
2. Alberta - Description and travel — 1981--
Guidebooks.   I. Title.

GV776.15.A4L89   1997   797.1'22'0971233   C97-900624-4

Published by:

Mark Lund
5404 - 114 A St.
Edmonton, Alberta
T6H 3M7

e-mail: lundm@planet.eon.net

Photographs by Mark Lund   (except as noted)
Edited by Lois Samis Lund
Production by Mark Lund

1st Printing - 1000 copies

Printed and Bound in Canada

Mark's Guide for Central Alberta Paddlers: Home Page
       http://www.planet.eon.net/~lundm/mgfcap1.html
       - for revisions and additions

"... no paddler has ever drowned on the portage trail."

DISCLAIMER

The various authors of the material contained within this guide have taken care to insure that the material is accurate, BUT, we humans are prone to error and conditions do change. **All paddlers must take full responsibility for insuring their own safety**. ALL PADDLERS must take advance precautions to insure that all their equipment is in good working order, and that any trip undertaken is taken at a safe water level and is within their paddling capabilities and the capabilities of the group with whom they paddle. While on the water each paddler must continuously evaluate the water, the rapids, and the weather, and determine if they have the ability to continue on a trip, or run a particular rapid, drop or other natural or man-made hazard. All trip participants should review and seriously consider the ***Safety Code of the American Whitewater Affiliation*** that is included within this guide as Appendix A.

Acknowledgments

Any project, even a small guide like this, is not done without assistance. I would like to acknowledge the previous work of my many colleagues from the *Canoe Alberta* projects of 1972 & '73, Bernice Parry for her work with the 1978 *Canoe Alberta* revisions, and the work of various Alberta Wilderness Association and Alberta Canoe Association members that helped with the *Canoeing Alberta* (1985) edition. The American Whitewater Affiliation again graciously allowed the use of their Safety Code. Without the editing of my good wife Lois, this would be a much more difficult read. And, I must thank all those paddlers with whom I have paddled and shared the lakes and rivers of this province, and across Canada. I thank you all!

Contents

Introduction

Canoeing and Kayaking in Edmonton and Central Alberta

As one may expect in a province so blessed with rivers, creeks and lakes, the paddling sports are well developed. Within Edmonton and Central Alberta there is a wide variety of paddling opportunities: the small ponds of Hermitage Park, the wide open waters of Lake Wabamun, the many leisurely day runs on the North Saskatchewan, the modest spring white water runs on the Sturgeon and Lobstick rivers, the long multi-day trips possible on the Athabasca, the exciting white water of the upper Red Deer and Brazeau rivers. Quite a range of possibilities!

Within Edmonton we have four canoe clubs: the Ceyana Canoe Club, the Edmonton White Water Paddlers, Friends of the River and the North West Voyagers. Each club offers a variety of educational, tripping, racing and social programs: further information including executive contacts is noted in Appendix B. Other paddling opportunities are available through the Strathcona Wilderness Centre in the County of Strathcona, through YoWoChAs -- the YWCA camp on Lake Wabamun, and through Edmonton Parks and Recreation (now Community Services). The River Valley Centre (an Edmonton Parks and Recreation facility) in Rossdale, just west of the James MacDonald Bridge (on 97 Ave.), is a good place to begin a search for up-to-date program and club brochures. Totem Outdoor Outfitters on 99th street, and the University of Alberta Outdoor Centre (in the Butterdome) are both good locations for up-to-date information about paddling and outdoor clubs, programs, and equipment. Map Town on 100 Ave. & 108 St. is now the best Edmonton source for maps and guide books. Outside of Edmonton, in the smaller population centers such as Red Deer, Rocky Mountain House, Hinton and Jasper, smaller canoe clubs and commercial outlets are available to service the needs of local paddlers and tourists.

This Guide

Canoeing guides for Alberta have been an ongoing concern of mine since the late Herb Benthin first made the suggestion to me in 1971: *... what canoeing in this province really needs is a good canoe guide!* With Herb's prod, and the subsequent announcement of the 1972 *Opportunities for Youth* program, I was soon deep into researching and preparing the first version of *Canoe Alberta* with a group of college friends. Since then I have contributed to each subsequent version of *Canoe Alberta*, and Janice MacDonald's *Canoeing Alberta* (1985). In 1996 I self-published my first guide, *Mark's Guide for Edmonton Paddlers* and given its primitive and limited production, I was really happy to sell nearly 150 copies. Now in 1997, I have given that work a major overhaul and expanded its scope to a broad band across the centre of Alberta.

In 1996 I wrote that a canoe guide is never completed. Rivers, roads and other geographic features just change too quickly. But unlike in 1996, I now hope that this press run will last a few years, so that I and my family can get back to more real paddling, not this computer stifled version! Some of you may ask why I have chosen not to include all navigable waters within the region. Too much, too big! And, I have come to the conclusion that some people would like that "sense" of exploration, and so there are still rivers and lakes in central Alberta, for which you will have to do your own research, your own exploration.

I always look forward to comments and suggestions, for updated and new information, that I may incorporate into future editions. All submissions will be acknowledged in future editions, just as I have tried in this edition to acknowledge the contributions of Ted Bentley, Mel and Carol Kraft. All submissions may be made to me;

by mail: 5404 - 114 A St., Edmonton, Alberta, T6H 3M7
by e-mail: lundm@planet.eon.net

This is a guide to a selection of the rivers and lakes of central Alberta. It is not an instructional manual. I have included in Appendix B both the contact addresses for some of the canoe clubs, and the best sources of instructional programs in the area. In Appendix C I have listed some of the best paddling manuals that I have come across. If you are unsure of your paddling abilities, check a manual to learn what you should know. Then check into a paddling program to upgrade your skills. **Most paddling accidents can be attributed to either poor skill,** or **poor judgement!** Please try to avoid both! And again, the reports in this guide do vary in quality, most reports are based on numerous runs by myself and/or other experienced paddlers. However I have also kept a few that are based on more sketchy information — these reports are so noted and any such runs taken should be considered exploratory -- allow more time and a greater margin of skill!

How to Use This Guide

This guide can be used for the planning of canoe trips of a few hours or of many days in length. This guide has been written conservatively, both with consideration to grading and classification of rivers and rapids, and to the time-distance estimates. New paddlers to the rivers of this guide, or novice paddlers should start with the smaller, low gradient streams, then work your way up in both gradient and volume. Each reach report lists gradients and volumes and you will soon come to recognize those that match your skills. In addition each report suggests the required level of skill. How do your skills measure up? The hardest thing to consider is when should a river trip be canceled because of high water. These reports, and our provincial stream flow forecast center, describe flows between the 25th and 75th percentile as normal flows, and these generally should not be a concern. Once stream volumes exceed about the 75th percentile for early summer, and/or the stream or river is brimming or overflowing the normal banks, the hydraulics within the stream become dangerous, even on little rivers and creeks. Above normal (for early summer) volumes are dangerous and paddlers should consider canceling or changing their trip to another run. But do remember, that there is always a 50% chance that the river volumes will be reported as below or above normal -- the key is the early summer (flood season) "normal" volumes.

River volumes are recorded in "cubic meters per second" or "CMS." Small rivers like the Wildhay, may be a fun paddle at 20 CMS, or a medium sized river like the Red Deer at Red Deer may require 40 CMS as a minimum, or an even larger stream like the North Saskatchewan 150 CMS is a minimal flow, but, at 1000 CMS the North Saskatchewan can become dangerous. Flow reports are published weekly by the River Forecast Center and are available on the Stream Flow Line, through the Alberta Rite # 310-0000 -*wait for instructions*- 207-2718.

Stream gradients for the reports in this guide are provided as meters per kilometer (m/km). Big rivers like the North Saskatchewan in Edmonton flow along quite nicely at .5 m/km, whereas smaller foothill streams like the Red Deer are exciting white water at 7 to 8 m/km. With more volume, less gradient is required to make exciting, or even dangerous rapids!

Novice paddlers should recognize that rivers are "graded" over the whole reach, and rapids are "classified" based on the **easiest** run through — not the biggest "hole." Generally class III water is considered the limit of an open canoe, especially when tripping — some white water jocks will contest this, and succeed, but not every time!

Within the various reports I have noted convenient public and commercial campgrounds, and made some suggestions regarding "wilderness" sites. But, some people can camp anywhere, and some only at the Banff Springs Hotel! Consider your needs, preferences, size of your group, and season, before planning to camp along many of the reaches in this guide. In the most of this province, at normal flows one or two tents can camp just about anywhere. Large groups must be more careful.

This guide should be but one tool in your planning for a trip. I encourage you to buy at least one set of up-to-date maps for any paddle. Most of the following reports will recommend a number of maps; they are all not necessary. And if you are leading a group, especially novices, take a "scouting" trip in advance. Leaders should know where they are going, how long it will take, and be able to anticipate most problems! Like the Scout motto;
Be Prepared!

Edmonton Area Rivers and Lakes

North Saskatchewan River - Drayton Valley to Devon

Duration of Tour(s)
*134 km
Drayton Valley to Devon or even on to Edmonton can be
done as a four to five day paddle. When the Klondike Days
Canoe race was a professional marathon race, Drayton to
Devon, 134 km, was one day of a three day race!
This reach of the North Saskatchewan makes possible a
number of half, full day, and overnight trips.

59th Edmonton Scouts, below Berrymoor Bridge,
September '97

Classification
1. Overall River:	Grade 1 with possibly some grade 2 between Berrymoor Bridge and Genesse Natural Area	
2. Rapids: water levels	Class I to easy Class II at most	
3. Skill of Paddlers:	Novice with basic strokes and river skills on all reaches. Inexperienced paddlers will require good guidance on the Berrymoor to Genesse run, because logjams and sweepers can be frequent on this short stretch.	

Start
The upstream start for this reach is the Willey West campground on the east bank of the river, just below the
#39/22 Highway bridge. Access to the campground is approximately 2 km up the hill and east of the bridge. You
must drive right through the campground to reach the river access.

Intermediate Access and Distances

Location	km	km	Access &/or Comments
Willey West Campground	0.0		right bank
Berrymoor Bridge (#759)	25.6	25.6	
Old Ferry Access	25.8	0.2	either bank
Burtonsville Island Nat. Area	46.8	21.0	left bank / camping / poor access
Old Genesse Ferry Crossing	68.8	22.0	left bank
Genesse Bridge (# 770)	87.5	18.7	right bank
Honeyvale Acres rge.rd. 275	116.0	28.5	left bank
Devon Bridge (# 60)	130.2	14.2	either bank
Devon - River Valley Lions C.G.	134.0	3.8	right bank

Finish
This reach report finishes at the Devon, River Valley Lions Campground. Access is through the town of Devon on
Saskatchewan Avenue, and then down the hill and across the golf course. At the campground gate take the dirt
road to the left and follow it for 150 m down to the river. **Shuttles** for this run are easily made along highways
#39, #759, #770, #627 and #60

Gradient

Within this reach river gradient varies approximately from .3 to 1.8 m per km.

River Volume and Flow Rate
The North Saskatchewan is a good size river, exceeded in size by only the Slave, Peace and Athabasca rivers in Alberta. During the summer months of June and July the river volume averages approximately 400 CMS, with a normal range (25 to 75 percentile) of approximately 250 CMS to 700 CMS. The extreme range of volumes reported between 1956 and 1985 is from less than 100 CMS to more than 3000 CMS for June and sometimes July in Edmonton. Average volumes, and the range of volumes reported, is less during the spring, late summer and fall months. Low volumes are rarely a problem on this river. High volumes, FLOODS that are likely to required trip cancellation most often occur from early June to mid-July.

The rate of stream flow varies with volume, from less than 2 kmph with 100 CMS to 8 kmph with more than 2000 CMS.

Maps
- West Edmonton Reprographics (1993) Edmonton Area Land Use Map 1:100,000
- an up-to-date Provincial Highways Map
- National Topographic Survey 1:250,000 -- 83 G Wabamun, 83 H Edmonton
- up-to-date county maps, County of Parkland, County of Leduc and the Brazeau Municipal District

Camping
Public campgrounds are available at Willey West Campground at Drayton Valley, and the River Valley Lions Campground in Devon. Wilderness campsites can be found on this reach. Over the whole run there are islands that at medium to low water levels can provide camping for smaller parties. There are some larger islands such as Burtonsville (a provincial Natural Area) that can handle very large groups, but these are the exception.

River Notes
Dratyon Valley to Edmonton is a classic, first multi-night trip, for many Edmonton area paddlers. In recent years the river valley west of Devon has become more pastoral, but the many islands, and the steepness and depth of the river valley still provide a good sense of leaving civilization behind. The river is home to much wildlife, and spotting bald eagles, deer, coyotes, cliff swallows, beavers and moose is still the norm over a multi-day trip.

The *Atlas of Alberta* and the old *Canoe Alberta* report a number of short-lived fur trade posts on this reach: Quagmire House just upstream of the Berrymoor Bridge, Buck Lake House opposite the mouth of Buck Lake (Modeste) Creek and a series of Upper Whitemud Houses in the vicinity of the confluence with Wabamun Creek.

As a paddling instructor and Scout leader, one run that I have often used is from Berrymoor Bridge to the Old Genesse ferry crossing, camping overnight on Burtonsville Island. On other occasions with less proficient paddlers, I have spent part of the first day developing paddling skills on the snye along the north side of Burtonsville Island. Then for the late afternoon, we have tracked our boats upstream (like the old voyagers) to the canoe campsite on the SE corner of the island. Then on the second day, we have completed the paddle down to the former ferry crossing. These are short weekend trips, and require only a Saturday morning departure, and generally put you home for supper on Sunday. But the unexpected can happen: one time on the second day we had just come around the bend below the Genesse Power Plant water intake, and such a forceful cold front blew in that we had to drag our boats down the river on ropes to the next bend, where the great breeze became a tail wind.

North Saskatchewan River — Devon to Fort Saskatchewan

Duration of Tour(s)
* 79.7 km

Devon to Edmonton, and Edmonton to the "Fort" can each be done as ½ day paddles, though the whole trip could easily be spread out over two or more days. There are many access points, on both sides of the river, and many shorter paddles are available. Devon to Whitemud Park is maybe the most popular Sunday afternoon paddle in the Edmonton area.

Looking back at the Beverly Bridges

Classification
1. Overall River: Grade 1
2. Rapids: Class I
3. Skill of Paddlers: Novice with basic strokes and river skills.

Start
This reach report starts at the Devon River Valley Lions Campground. Access is through the town of Devon on Saskatchewan Avenue and then down the hill and across the golf course. At the campground gate take the dirt road to the left and follow it for 150 m down to the river.

Intermediate Access and Distances

Location	km	km	Access &/or Comments
Devon - River Valley Lions C.G.	0.0		right bank
Big Island	14.5	14.5	left bank / camping / no access
River Ridge Golf Course	15.0	0.5	right bank
Terwiliger Park*	23.5	8.5	right bank / 500 m portage
Whitemud Park & Creek	28.8	5.3	right bank
Laurier Park access**	29.8	1.0	left bank
Emily Murphy Park	34.7	4.9	right bank
Rafters Landing***	39.7	5.0	right bank
Dawson Park	42.2	2.5	left bank
Capilano Park / 50 St.**	46.1	3.9	right bank
Hermitage Park	53.0	6.9	left bank / 150 m portage
Twp. Rd. 540 / C.R. Sewage Plant	63.3	10.3	right bank
Fort Saskatchewan / Riverside Pk.	79.7	16.4	right bank

* The Terwilliger Park launch usually requires a portage of 500 m or so, unless you have a group and are able to make arrangements with Edmonton Parks and Recreation (now Community Services) for a gate key. These arrangements (spring 1997) can be initiated by calling the River Valley Centre at 496-7275.

** Laurier Park and 50 Street are the two access points in Edmonton where at most water levels you can drive right down to the water edge for loading and unloading.

*** With the new riverboat moored at Rafters Landing, this may not be as useful an access point as it has been.

Finish

In Fort Saskatchewan, possibly the best access, is the second access point east, along River Road just above the island. River Road is accessed by taking 101 Street north from Highway #15, and where 101 Street meets the river it becomes River Road.

Gradient

Within this reach river gradient varies approximately from .3 to .9 m per km.

River Volume and Flow Rate

The North Saskatchewan is a good size river, exceeded in size by only the Slave, Peace and Athabasca rivers in Alberta. During the summer months of June and July the river volume averages approximately 400 CMS, with a normal range (25 to 75 percentile) of approximately 250 CMS to 700 CMS. The extreme range of volumes reported between 1956 and 1985 is from less than 100 CMS to more than 3000 CMS for June and sometimes July, in Edmonton. Weekly average volumes, and the range of volumes reported, is less during the spring, late summer and fall months. Low volumes are rarely a problem on this river. High volumes, FLOODS that are likely to required trip cancellation most often occur from early June to mid-July.

The rate of stream flow varies with volume, from less than 2 kmph with 100 CMS to 8 kmph with more than 2000 CMS.

Maps

- West Edmonton Reprographics (1993) Edmonton Area Land Use Map 1:100,000
- an up-to-date Provincial Highways Map
- National Topographic Survey 83 H Edmonton
- up-to-date county map for Strathcona County

Camping

Public campgrounds are available at the start in Devon, and off the river, at the Rainbow Valley Campground in Edmonton. Youth groups are able to make arrangements through the River Valley Center (496-7275) to utilize *Big Island* on the western boundary of Edmonton for overnight camping. There are also some rather barren islands upstream of Fort Saskatchewan that could be used for camping.

River Notes

At normal flows these reaches of this river are all considered to be safe runs for paddlers with basic paddling and river skills, and even for beginner lessons with good instructors. The North Saskatchewan is a large enough river that on hot sunny afternoons it will generate its own upstream breeze. It is best to plan for morning trips! Access outside of the above noted points is often difficult due to the high muddy banks and private property restrictions.

Our river is often remote from the hustle and bustle of the city through which it flows. Wildlife is abundant and it is usual to spot beaver, muskrat, deer, fox, coyotes and a great variety of bird life. On occasion even moose and bear maybe spotted on the fringes of the city. The river is a noted pickerel fishery, often provides up ling cod (suckers), goldeye and infrequently lake sturgeon.

Our river valley is an excellent means to view the history of the area. The valley sides display the geological foundation for the region. Coal seams can be seen at various points along the way. The record of the last glaciation can be seen in the tills and remnants of the deltas and meltwater channels. More recent history can viewed as one passes Fort Edmonton, the remnants of John Walters ferry just above 105 St. Bridge, the right-of-way scar of the *Edmonton, Yukon & Pacific Railway* above Victoria Park, and the reworked coal mine and gravel pits that have become Terwilliger, Harwelak, Kinsmen, Rundle and other parks.

North Saskatchewan River - Fort Saskatchewan to Victoria Settlement

Duration of Tour(s)
* 80.3 km
Fort Saskatchewan to Victoria Settlement can be completed as a very easy long weekend tour (3 days), and within this reach there are a number of half and full day paddles.

Classification
1. Overall River: Grade 1
2. Rapids: Class I
3. Skill of Paddlers: Novice with basic strokes and river skills.

Pelicans below Fort Saskatchewan

Start
The proposed start for this trip is the second access point along River Road in Fort Saskatchewan, just above the island. River Road is accessed by taking 101 Street north from Highway #15, and where 101 Street meets the river it becomes River Road.

Intermediate Access and Distances

Location	km	km	Access &/or Comments
Fort Saskatchewan - River Rd.	0		south / right Bank
Fort Augustus	1.5	1.5	historic monument / poor access
New Railway Bridge	4.8	3.3	not on most maps / poor access
Pump House / Rge. Rd. 215	14.8	10	right bank
Vinca Bridge # 38	26	11.2	left bank
Waskatenau Bridge # 831	52.1	26.1	either bank
#855 Bridge S. of Smoky Lake	74.7	22.6	very poor access
Victoria Settlement / Prov. Hist. Site	80.3	5.6	left bank at old ferry crossing

Finish
Victoria Settlement, south-east of Smoky Lake may be reached by taking Victoria Trail, east off of highway #855, just north of the bridge over the river. In Victoria Settlement follow the old road down to the river at the old ferry crossing, immediately south of the historic site. **Shuttles** for this run are possible along highways #15, #830, #38, #45, #831, #855 and the old Victoria Trail on the north bank for the last reach.

Gradient, Flow Rate and River Volume
Alberta Environment has not published flow rate and volume data for the North Saskatchewan below Edmonton. So please refer to the previous reports for this data. The river does gain some volume along the way and is a little larger by the time it reaches Victoria Settlement.

This is a flat run; gradients vary between .3 and .6 m/km.

Maps
- an up-to-date provincial highways map
- National Topographic Survey 83 H Edmonton, and 83 I Tawatinaw
- county maps: Municipal District of Sturgeon, County of Lamont, County of Thorhild, County of Smoky Lake and Strathcona County

Camping
My wife Lois and I paddled this run in August of '96, and we found campsites a little scarce. There are some islands in the river, especially just below the Vinca Bridge and we were able to make do with grassy points below the high water mark. There are no commercial or other public campgrounds along the river on these reaches.

River Notes
In August '96 Lois and I completed two paddles as research for this edition of the guide, Maligne Lake and this run. Maligne Lake has spectacular scenery but this run had the wildlife. We actually started right in Edmonton and made it to Smoky Lake in three easy days, but we were blessed with tail winds and sailed all but 24 km. Even before we had left Edmonton we had spotted a half a dozen deer, beaver and a fox. There was a peregrine falcon perched on the Fort Saskatchewan Highway #15 bridge. And, by the time we reached Victoria Settlement we had seen a wide variety of birdlife including eagles, and each day a flock of pelicans. Hawks were almost continuously soaring over the river, and we watched at least one osprey take a fish from the river. On Maligne Lake we had to share the lake with the commercial tour boats, and many other paddlers — on this run we had the river to ourselves. When passing through the Lobstick Settlement, one local was so amazed to see us sailing by that he ran down to the waters edge to wave, and later his wife stopped to talk to us at Victoria Settlement. She confirmed our observations that pelicans are more numerous these days than in past years.

We suspect that people do not tackle these runs in great numbers because they believe them to be unpleasant due to pollution. NOT the case! Yes there is a little smell in the immediate vicinity of the wastewater plants, and we would not drink the water, but there is very little observable evidence of pollution anywhere along the river. Again, a note of caution: the provincial fisheries guide does suggest that fish consumption from the river be restricted and avoided by pregnant women. This is a very pleasant paddle, one I'll do again, and even take along a few more friends next time.

Other Reaches
This river can be paddled (with a few portages around dams) all the way to Lake Winnipeg! There are many more pleasant runs, we suspect, downstream of Victoria Settlement, and the bridges are almost each a one day paddle apart, all the way to the Saskatchewan border. Dig out the road map, the topo' sheets and get going!!

Sturgeon River - Bon Accord to the North Saskatchewan

Duration of Tour(s)
* 36 km

These reaches of the Sturgeon make possible a number of short half-day, full day, and even overnight trips. This report covers the most popular spring training run on the Sturgeon, the run between Bon Accord and Gibbons, and a number of other pleasant tours.

Willie - Spring Surfing!

Classification
1. Overall River   Grade 1 to 1+
2. Rapids   Class 1 to 2
3. Skill of Paddlers   Novice Paddlers with basic strokes and some knowledge and skill with basic river maneuvers.

Start
The upper run of the reaches reported here commences approximately 5.5 km south of Bon Accord on Rge. Rd. 240. On all the country roads here, be sure to pull your vehicle as far into the ditch as possible when loading, unloading and leaving your vehicle. For this run Edmonton paddlers often meet at North Town Mall, or in Bon Accord. The easiest approach is Highway 28 to Bon Accord and then south.

Intermediate Access and Distances

Location	km	km	Access &/or Comments
Rge. Rd. 240 - S. of Bon Accord	0.0		right bank
Rge. Rd. 234 - W. of Gibbons	8.2	8.2	left bank
Gibbons Bridge	12.2	4.0	either bank
Rge. Rd. 231 - E. of Gibbons	15.9	3.7	left bank
Sec. Highway 643 - E. of Gibbons	18.4	2.5	either bank
Sec. Highway 825 - N. of Ft. Sask.	29.0	10.6	left bank
Rge. Rd. 222 - N. of Ft. Sask.	35.4	6.4	left bank

Finish
The finish of this run is most easily reached by taking Secondary Highway 825 north from Fort Saskatchewan (off Highways 15 & 37), then east on to Twp. Rd. 552. Follow this road as it first bends to the N.E. and then east again to meet Rge. Rd. 222, just where it crosses the Sturgeon. The river is quite deeply incised at this point and the access does require a good hike down to the water. The best parking is on the east side and off the main road, near a microwave tower. **Shuttles** for this river require a detailed map. I have suggested one below.

Gradient
These runs on the Sturgeon offer gradients ranging from 0.67 m/km for the run just downstream of Gibbons, to as high as 1.7 m/km for the run just above and through Gibbons. The last run down to Rge. Rd. 222 offers the second highest gradient of 1.5 m/km.

River Volume and Flow Rate

Stream flows for the Sturgeon have not been published. The river is generally considered to be a "spring training run" for Edmonton white water paddlers. It is generally run in late April and early May each year. Local paddlers have also reported good paddling after long and heavy rainstorms. Beware of any flow that threatens to overflow the normal banks.

Maps

- NTS 1:50,000: 83H14 - Redwater
- West Edmonton Reprographics (1993) Edmonton Area Land Use Map 1:100,000 (good for **shuttle** planning!)

Camping

To date in my runs along the upper two reaches of this report, and through my travels in the area I have not discovered any commercial or public campgrounds along the river. All of the lands adjacent to this river are privately owned -- and many of the owners are very protective of their holdings. One should make camping arrangements before commencing on an overnight trip on this reach of the Sturgeon. The recommended Land Use Map above and a current phone book may help you to reach land owners along the river.

River Notes

Over the years Ceyana paddlers have always considered the upper reach included in this report as "the spring run!" My own experience is limited to the upper two reaches. Local paddlers from along the river have always used other reaches, and recently I have learned of various school groups taking extended trips along all of the Sturgeon from Big Lake to the confluence.

Many sections of the river are very pretty with heavy growths of spruce along the banks, others sections wind through willow and oxbow flats where poplar, birch and rose bushes line the banks. Some sections of this river take you well away from the homes of the local acreages and for short periods the river can almost convince one that you are paddling a wilderness stream, and then the next bend will bring you right through a farm yard or an acreage development. Beware! One of the greater hazards along these reaches maybe the **barbed wire fences** that some farmers occasionally stretch across a corner of a bend, or even across the whole river at low water to keep their cattle in. Log jams have been known to come and go on these reaches, and some of the bridges and culverts that the river flows through can become plugged with debris. But, the beaver dams are far more likely to provide the excitement of your trip. Some springs they provide enough of a drop that the "white water jocks" can even practise a little surfing below each dam, or "crank" some great turns on the "jets."

Whitemud Creek - from 23 Ave to the North Saskatchewan

Duration of Tour(s)
* 12 km

These reaches of the Whitemud Creek make possible two short tours: the upper run is 8 km and can take 2 to 3 hours, the lower run is 4 km and can take one to two hours to finish.

Classification
1. Overall River   Grade 1+
2. Rapids   Class 1 - 2
3. Skill of Paddlers   Novice

Unfortunately we tend to run Whitemud only when the water is high or in flood. High water makes the grading scheme difficult to apply because the "hydraulics" relative to the stream channel and flow can make it more dangerous than immediately apparent, especially at constrictions and at the log jams that often form. Whitemud **has drowned** unwary paddlers in the past! We also tend to paddle it only in the early spring when skills are a little rusty, and the water is cold. The high muddy water and narrow channels can make both self and assisted rescues difficult. At high water the creek is deep right into the willows! For new paddlers, it, like many mountain streams is best paddled with experience paddlers who have been "down" recently. Once the spring flood, or post-storm high water crest has passed and the stream flow has begun to drop significantly, then less experienced paddlers can begin to poke, pole and drag their way down.

Start
The upper access for these two runs is on the south side of 23 Avenue in S.W. Edmonton. Park in the parking area about 125 m east of the bridge, portage down and put in between the old bridge and the new bridge. This access provides an 8 km run down to Snow Valley.

Intermediate Access and Distances
Rainbow/Snow Valley off Whitemud Freeway is 4 km from the mouth of the creek. Park in the Snow Valley lot and pull out or put in, just upstream of the little bridge.

Finish
Whitemud Creek flows into the North Saskatchewan about 400 m below Quesnel Bridge on Whitemud Freeway. Access to Whitemud Creek and Park is off Fox Drive, just east of the Fox Drive Bridge; turn north, avoid the Equine Centre road, and follow Keillor Road around and into the park right near the creek confluence. **Shuttles** may be driven along 23 Ave., 119/122 St., Rainbow Valley Rd., Belgravia Road, Fox Drive, and Keillor Road.

Gradient
The highest gradients computed for this run occur for one short interval in the middle of the upper run, 7.8 m/km, with other intervals ranging from 0.7 m/km to 6.8 m/km. I expect that the contour lines on this reach are far from perfect and some of these higher gradients are in reality spread out a little more evenly. The upper run is the more exciting of the two. The lower run has computed gradients of 1.2 & 1.6 m/km -- and is a far more leisurely paddle. These distances and gradients were computed using the 1:25,000 sheets, with a 10 foot or 3.1 m contour interval.

River Volume and Flow
This is generally a spring flood or post-big storm run, for a couple of weeks if we are lucky in April and then a few days some summers. I have not been able to find published flow or velocity data for Whitemud Creek.

Maps
- a up-to-date Edmonton street map
- NTS (1:25,000); 83H /5h Whitemud Creek, and 83H /12a Dunvegan Yards.

Camping
Public camping is available in Rainbow Valley Campground, right on the Creek!

River Notes
Whitemud Creek is well named. One generally brings home a little light colored clay gumbo each run. Either run is usually a good opportunity to see beavers, to enjoy their dams (the best drops) and view their use of the Balsam Poplars that line this creek. The beavers are also the major contributor of trees to the logjams and sweepers that paddlers must contend with. The upper run reported here is through one of the more wilderness-like ravines in Edmonton; in places it is more than 500 m wide. The ravine is home to many deer, coyotes, fox, skunks, and a wide variety of bird life. In many places the north-facing slopes still have good stands of spruce and birch, and the south-facing banks have stands of balsam poplar with a heavy understory of alder, red-ossier dogwood and rose bushes. In recent years the park has been upgraded with bridges, lots of clearance at most water levels, and a major graveled path up the middle, with connecting paths to the many neighborhoods.

The old snow dump gravels still make a gentle and secure river access at Whitemud Park for both the creek and the river. I understand from some older paddlers this was not always the case, and I have observed that since the ending of snow dumping here, the bank has become steeper as the river erodes more of the gravel away each spring. In time the "city" may have to do a little work to maintain this fine access.

Other Runs
I have detailed only the two most common runs here. Local adventuresome paddlers, including myself, have at times attacked the higher reaches on both Whitemud and Blackmud creeks. They both can be logjam, beaver dammed runs that require optimal timing for the right volume.

Astotin Lake — Elk Island National Park

Astotin Lake is within Elk Island National Park. The lake may be reached by taking Highway #16 east from Edmonton, and then north on the main park roadway. The lake is in the northern third of the park, on the west side of the recreation and camping area. From the main parking lot it is a short portage of 100 m or so down to the beach and launching. Astotin Lake is a skewed, tear-dropped shaped lake, nearly 2 km on the long axis and over 1.5 km at its widest. The south half of the lake has many islands and bays. The lake makes an excellent day trip. Because of the islands the south half is largely sheltered and a great place to initiate new paddlers. Astotin is a wonderful location for birding. For many years the late Bob Turner would lead a Ceyana Canoe Club trip each spring just for the birding. In recent years the Park has closed the lake to paddlers each fall (September to freeze-up) to reduce pressure on the migrating Trumpeter Swans. You may confirm this closure by calling the Park Warden's Office at 992 - 2950. There has also been discussion about closing the middle section of the parkway, which will mean that Astotin will only be accessible from the north, off Highway #15, and south just west of Lamont.

Islet Lake -- Cooking Lake -- Blackfoot Recreation Area

Islet Lake is located in the south-central portion of the Cooking Lake -- Blackfoot Recreation Area, approximately 40 minutes or so east of Edmonton. Access to the Islet Lake Staging Area is via Sherwood Park Freeway, through "the Park," and then continue on Wye Road past North Cooking Lake. The first Provincial Park signs for Islet and Central Staging areas appear just beyond North Cooking Lake; follow these signs for another 12 - 15 minutes to reach Islet Lake.

Islet Lake is a smallish lake, approximately 3 km long and nearly 1 km wide at its greatest. The lake has many little bays, one large island, and some smaller islets. The S.W. shore has a small acreage development. The east side is mostly within the Provincial Recreation Area. A walking/biking/ski trail follows the east shore. The staging area has good parking and a very nice picnic site with a wood-stove heated shelter. The lake is very sheltered, a wonderful place for new paddlers to practise, and a great place for viewing wildlife. Locals have reported even spotting Pelicans feeding on Islet in late June, but we suspect that the only significant fish population maybe sticklebacks.

Hermitage Ponds — Hermitage Park in Edmonton

Hermitage Ponds are a series of three small spring-fed lakes in Hermitage Park, in N.E. Edmonton. They may be reached via Yellowhead Trail, north onto Victoria Trail and then east onto Hermitage Road. Follow Hermitage Road right down and into the park. Turn left at the "T" in the park and follow the road between the ponds and use the north parking lot. The most easterly pond is the largest and contains two small islands. Now that the trees in the park are beginning to reach maturity these ponds are becoming a very nicely sheltered paddling spot. These are the only ponds in the city that paddlers can freely access. All other stormwater ponds are generally closed due to poor water quality. Hermitage Ponds are probably the best spot within the city for those first few tentative paddling strokes, before tackling the river. Hermitage is stocked with trout most years, and provincial fishing regulations do apply.

Chickakoo Lake - County of Parkland

Chickakoo Lake is a well sheltered kettle lake in the moraine north and west of Stony Plain. Chickakoo Lake may be reached by taking Secondary Highway #779, 3.2 km north from Highway #16X (turn at the church), then 4.1 km west on Twp.Rd. #534, then north 1.6 km, and finally, turn right (east) and follow along the south shore of Chickakoo Lake to the county recreation area, parking lot and boat launch. The county has made major improvements to this park in recent years and the recreation area has some very nice picnic facilities, wheel chair assessable outhouses and well graveled boat launch, with lots of parking. Chickakoo is relatively deep into the kettle and is surrounded by a mature aspen forest, which makes for a nicely sheltered paddle from all but the strongest winds. Chickakoo is a small lake with a number of interesting bays, and an abundance of wildlife. With its fine picnic facilities it makes for a very nice evenings paddle for Edmonton area residents.

Hasse Lake — Hasse Lake Provincial Park

Hasse Lake is a "day use" Provincial Park some 40 minutes west of the city. It may be reached via Highway #16 through Stony Plain. Approximately 7 km beyond Stony Plain take the Edmonton Beach road west for 2.4 km, and then turn south for 3.3 km, and then turn west and follow a winding road for some 5 km. The route is well signed once past Edmonton Beach.

The park is on the northwest shore of Hasse lake, and provides piers, a playground, picnic shelter, water pump and walking trails. Hasse Lake is nearly 1.5 km long, and almost a kilometer wide, with two islands. It reaches a depth of over 9 m, but is largely a "soft" shore lake with just a small beach within the park. Along the west side of the lake are three sheltered bays. The lake has "spring fed," relatively clean water with a low "nutrient loading." Hasse supports a sport fishery of rainbow trout through regular stocking. The lake has had a history of winter kills. One unusual aspect of the Hasse Lake fishery, has been the introduction of the "Threespine Stikleback" by persons unknown (an illegal activity). Hasse Lake is generally a quiet spot, boat speed is restricted to 12 km/hr on the whole lake. Hasse is a larger "kettle" along the eastern edge of the Duffield Moraine that provides a great spot for an afternoon paddle, a little fishing, or even some "birding."

The Jasper to Hinton region — rivers and lakes

Athabasca River - Athabasca Falls to Jasper / Old Fort Point Bridge

Duration of Tour
* 31.8 km
This reach can be done as a long days paddle, or broken nicely into three shorter ½ day paddles.

Contemplating the outflow from below the Falls!

Classification
1. Overall River: Grade 2
2. Rapids: Class II to III
3. Skill of Paddlers: Intermediate paddlers with strong white water skills for both the upper and lower reach. The middle reach can be tackled by intermediate paddlers with weaker skills, if under the guidance of one experienced with the run. Both the put-ins, for the upper and lower runs, have been posted by Parks Canada with signs, NOT RECOMMENDING the run be tackled by open canoes. When the glaciers are running, and the river is full, both of these runs require good skills, canoes filled with floatation, and paddlers prepared to swim in the cold glacier water.

Start
Access to this run is just north of Athabasca Falls off, of Highway #93A. Use the Geraldine Lakes trailhead parking lot. Then portage across the highway and down an old road/trail to the river and put-in at the pool at the bottom of the gorge below the falls.

Intermediate Access and Distances

Location	km	km	Access &/or Comments
Athabasca Falls - pool below	0		left bank
Kerkeslin Creek / rapid	3.3	3.3	no access
Highway #93	9.1	5.8	right bank
Meeting of the Waters / Whirlpool	11.8	2.7	left bank / off of #93 A
Rafters put-in	12.2	0.4	right bank / off of #93
Mile 5 Bridge	23.5	11.3	left bank / off of #93
Beckers Bungalows / rapid	25.8	2.3	
Old Fort Point / Jasper / Bridge	31.8	6	right bank

Finish
Old Fort Point is directly south of Jasper. Use the middle access road into Jasper from Highway #16. Instead of turning into Jasper, turn south, and then take the next left, and head east, down to and across the river. There is a large parking lot next to the big pool just below the bridge on the east or right bank. Please park away from the river beach after dropping off your canoe, because the commercial rafters arrive very frequently during the tourist season. **Shuttles** for this run are made along highways #93, #93A, #16 and the local road down to Old Fort Point bridge.

Gradient

The individual average gradients on this reach vary from just below 3 m/km to nearly 7 m/km. As with many whitewater reaches I suspect they do average out a little!

River Volume and Flow Rate

During the summer months normal flows on this reach, at Jasper, vary from 150 cms to 380 cms with mid July mean of 250 cms. Peak flows may exceed 650 cms. Velocities vary from less than 2 km/hr at 30 cms to 7 km/hr at 350 cms. Flow rates will vary considerably on this run, and the hydrology station is located approximately 2 km above the finish.

Maps

- NTS 1:50,000: 83C/12 Athabasca Falls, 83C/13 Medicine Lake, and 83D/16 Jasper
- Parks Canada 1:250,000 Jasper National Park
- Map Town Publishing 1:100,000 Jasper & Maligne Lake (my choice, but shows only Beckers and Wapiti rapid, no others!)

Camping

Numerous public campsites are available in Jasper National Park, and one must often take what is available. For groups, such as canoe clubs or youth groups, the park does maintain a "limited services" group site on the Whirlpool river, just off of #93A, a kilometer or two above the confluence with the Athabasca. This campsite can be booked through the Park Visitor Services unit (Park Information is 403-852-6161). Wapiti and Wabasso campgrounds are also situated along the river and both have some limited access to it. These campgrounds may have an advance reservation system in place. There are no "backcountry" campsites along this reach of the Athabasca.

River Notes

For us open boat paddlers, this is river paddling at Alberta's finest! Challenging, Scenic, and few highway intrusions. What more could one ask for? Do note, the "Falls" run, and the "Beckers" run are NOT RECOMMENDED for open canoes, and DO require good skill levels. I have made some awfully long rescues on both these sections, or, some paddlers have had some long cold swims! But if you are equipped with the skills and boats, go for it!

The first section has an impressive start. The pool at the bottom of the gorge below the falls, swirls and boils, and hisses with highly aerated water. This run can be intimidating, there is no time to warm-up, at most water levels you are immediately into a long class II to III rapid, all the way to commencement of the next canyon, over 500 m. Once into the canyon the river is a mix of long quiet pools interspersed with a series of rapids. The best or biggest drops occur at Kerkeslin and Hardisty creeks. Various authors, including myself, would suggest at some water levels both of these drops can go "good" class III (good means big, from an open canoe perspective!). Kerkeslin in particular has earned a reputation because of the calm pool above, the horizon line, and the echoing of the rapid roar up the canyon walls. Kerkeslin can be scouted from the right shore unless the river is in flood (not a good time to be there!).

There are two long stretches of rock garden - pushy - wet waves on this reach, one just above and below the first appearance of Highway #93 (km 9.1), and the other just below the confluence with the Whirlpool (km 11.8).

Small rapids, and gravel chutes occur regularly all along this reach. Between the Whirlpool and Mile 5 Bridge the most common "swimming" spot is "Dunk" corner (km 20). At this point the river makes a sweeping left turn, drops over a partial ledge and then a sharp right turn. The drop on the outside is considerable at most water levels, and the powerful boils "down the middle" usually require both some forward momentum, and a good brace.

Below Mile 5 Bridge again is not recommended for open canoes. The first rapid of significance occurs at Becker's Bungalows and can go class III (km 25.8). The whole stretch then down to km 29 is a series of rapids, often with large standing waves. The most complex rapid is opposite Wapiti Campground.

I have many, many fond memories of this reach and have used it for teaching and training many new paddlers. Possibly one of my best memories is the first time down. In '72 while with *Canoe Alberta* we hooked up with the local paddlers, Bryn Thomas and Ron Steer. At that time they were offering commercial klepper kayak tours of the Falls run and offered to take us along. Their hype had been such that I ended up paddling a kayak, and because my spray cover tended to leak, I thought, foolishly, that maybe a little Vaseline would help to water proof it. I was first into my boat and while waiting for the others made the mistake of resting my paddle on my spray cover. And thus I paddled the run with a very slippery shaft, and with my arms stretched out to the side so that I could grip the blades to maintain proper blade orientation. The second good reason for never forgetting the run was that after commencement, and into the canyon, Bryn and Ron stopped and searched each eddy. Only after starting did they mention that the wardens had asked them to look for the body of some unwary tourist who had backed into the falls while taking a picture. The body was found three months later near Whitecourt!

Like many park runs, this one can provide many wildlife viewing opportunities. Bear, moose and elk may be viewed almost anywhere on the run, and in the first canyon mountain sheep and goats have been observed. Historically this section of the river was not used by the voyagers as they usually traded their canoes for horses at Jasper House, east of Jasper Lake. Old Fort Point is probably a misnomer, as both Jasper and Henry Houses are usually reported as being to the east, and the name is usually ascribed to being a corruption of "old ford point."

Other Reaches

There is one other upstream run made regularly on the Athabasca, from the bend below Sunwapta Falls where the river meets the highway, down to Athabasca Falls. Parks Canada has developed a portage trail on the west/left bank around the falls, and conservative paddlers often take out along the highway a kilometer or so above the falls. There is a very good class III rapid above the falls -- it in **not** a good place to "mess around." This run is approximately 15 km long, includes a number of good class II rapids and a few will go class III at some water levels. Many of these rapids can be "wet and pushy" for open canoe paddlers. The river is generally a grade II stream with open gravel beaches. The gradient averages 4.8 m/km, with a maximum gradient of 6.8 m/km.

Athabasca River - Jasper to Whitecourt

Duration of Tour(s)
*306 km
This total tour could easily be spread out over two weeks, if one likes to fish and hike. It could also be done in as little as 5-6 days by paddlers prepared to push a little. Within this reach are many shorter part-day and multi-day trips.

Old Fort Point — looking downstream

Classification

1. Overall River:	Grade 2 with some long stretches of Grade 1
2. Rapids:	Class II
3. Skill of Paddlers:	Practised novice paddlers, with the basic river skills for ferrying and eddy turns

Start
Old Fort Point is directly south of Jasper. Use the middle access road into Jasper from Highway #16. Instead of turning into Jasper, turn south, and then take the next left, or head east down to and across the river. There is a large parking lot next to the big pool just below the bridge on the east or right bank. Please park away from the river beach after dropping off your canoe, the commercial rafters arrive very frequently during the tourist season.

Intermediate Access and Distances

Location	km	km	Access &/or Comments
Jasper / Old Fort Point Bridge	0.0		right bank
Maligne road bridge	4.9	4.9	right bank
Maligne River	8.0	3.1	right bank / access
Mile 12 Bridge / #16 E. of Jasper	21.6	13.6	left bank
Jasper Lake - N.E. shore / outlet	36.6	15.0	right bank
Disaster Point	40.2	3.6	right bank
Mouth of Solomon Creek	66.1	25.9	left bank
Old Entrance	76.0	9.9	left bank
Mouth of Maskuta Creek	81.3	5.3	right bank
Hinton Bridge	89.6	8.3	left bank
Obed Mine Bridge			access unknown
Old Obed Ferry Crossing	133.0	43.4	left bank
Emmerson Lakes Bridge	146.0	13.0	left bank
Pine Creek Gas Plant Bridge	199.3	53.3	left bank / Berland River confluence is just upstream
#947 Bridge	225.7	26.4	left bank
Windfall Gas Plant Bridge	269.5	43.8	right bank
Whitecourt / McLeod River	306.0	36.5	right bank

Finish

The finish in Whitecourt is off of #43, just south of the #43 bridge, turn east towards the McLeod River and follow the gravel road down to the confluence. This access is west of the main part of lower Whitecourt, and west of the #43 bridge over the McLeod River. **Shuttles** for these runs may involve highway #16, #40, the Brule Road, River Road in Hinton, the Emmerson Lakes haul road, the Pine Creek Gas Plant road, #947

Gradient

Much of this run falls at a rate between 1 and 2 m/km. Actual river gradient is a little higher, as both Jasper and Brule lake contribute some long flat stretches. There is one contour interval below the Emmerson Lakes Rd. bridge that appears much steeper, but from the water this appears to be an error.

River Volume and Flow Rate

The Athabasca is a big river, and grows on a long run such as reported here. In Hinton the "Athab'ee" averages about 500 cms in June and July, where as at Whitecourt it averages between 600 to 700 cms. At Whitecourt the Athabasca has a normal flow variation of between 400 and 850 cms in the summer months, and has had peak flows of over 2100 cms reported. Flow rates at Whitecourt vary from 1.5 km/hr at 300 cms to 9 km/hr at 3000 cms.

Maps

- NTS 1:50,000: 83 D/16 Jasper, 83 E/1 Snaring, 83 F/4 Miette, 83 F/5 Entrance (Jasper to Hinton only, best choice if planning to do side-trip hikes in the Park)
- NTS 1:250,000: 83 D Canoe River, 83 E Mt. Robson, 83 F Edson, 83 K Iosegun Lake, & 83 J Whitecourt
- Map Town Publishing 1:100,000 Jasper & Maligne Lake (if going for the long run, use this sheet plus 83 F, K & J above)
- Provincial Highways Map (essential)
- Alberta Forest Service — Edson Forest -- Recreation Areas and Trails map (good for up-to-date access)
- Alberta Forest Service — Whitecourt Forest -- Recreation Areas and Trails map (good for up-to-date access)

Camping

This is a river for tripping. Yes, there is at least one day trip below Jasper, but this is really a river for loading the canoe up an going camping, for a weekend, or two weeks. One problem is that there are only two primitive campsites where camping is permitted in Jasper Park, at km 24.6 on a island just above Jasper Lake (left bank, main channel), and just above the Fiddle river (km 53.3, right bank). Compounding this lack of allowed campsites within the park, is the regulation that groups must be less the 12 in number. To confirm these park regulations and to book a primitive campsite call the Trail Office at 403-852-6177. Once out of the park there are many nice campsites. I have used one near the head of Brule Lake on the east shore (km55.4), and another 2/3 of the way along the east shore at km 63. Both these sites are near small creeks. Once below Hinton there are many good campsites. I have earlier reported that the first Oldman Creek site has been abused in the past but as of a Fall '97 Ceyana Canoe Club trip the site appeared to have been cleaned up. I think we owe a thank-you to some good Samaritans.

There are numerous public campgrounds near this river, a number in Jasper Park, including Snaring River east of Jasper, Kinky/Wildhorse Lakes east of Brule Lake, in Hinton, at Emmerson Lakes and in Whitecourt.

River Notes

The runs in Jasper Park are fine scenic paddles. All of these runs in this report can be undertaken by semi-skilled novices, even with families, **at lower water levels**. The river can be a little tricky and bouncy at average summer flows, especially between Brule Lake and the Windfall Gas Plant Bridge. In the various stretches where the river is braided, logjams and sweepers are often a significant hazard. In late August '97 on a Ceyana Canoe Club trip, we found that the river has cut the meander bend just below Oldman Creek, and above the former gooseneck Rapid. This new channel was quite bouncy, with a strong current and many new sweepers. Beware and Be Alert as this is likely to remain such for at least the next couple of years. I especially like to return to the Athabasca in mid to late August, when the other rivers are starting run low on water.

Jasper to Hinton can be a long two-day paddle. Often to shorten the run, and to get out of the park with large groups, I have started at the Jasper Lake outlet, and then camped on Brule Lake, and then finished the second day in Hinton. The run below Jasper to Mile 12 Bridge has been a popular day run for Ceyana families. Emmerson Lakes Bridge to Whitecourt can make for a long three-day paddle, and for our '97 run mentioned above we pulled out at the Windfall Gas Plant bridge. Over the years many of us have avoided the first few miles immediately below the Hinton Pulp Mill due to the pollution, though this situation is improving.

When paddling these runs there are three historical points worth visiting. At about km 14 (right bank), just above Caronne creek are the remains of the Moberly buildings. John Moberly constructed this farmstead starting about 1898, and farmed here until 1910 when the government bought him out for the establishment of the park. At approximately km 38 (left bank) is the last site of Jasper's House, the longest lived fur trade post in the area. The meadow in the area can make for a pleasant walk. Along the east shore of Brule lake runs the abandoned railway line through a long series of sand dunes. At times the sand has buried the line to the depth of the telegraph posts, at others the wind has completely blown the railway bed away. Near the campsite at km 63 is an abandoned station that has been nearly covered by a sand dune.

Moberly Cabins (burned in the early '90's) km 14, Ceyana Canoe Club, 1985

The big eddy below "The Gates" km 190, Ceyana Canoe Club, September '97

Wildhay River — from above Highway #40 to above Jarvis Creek

Duration of Tour(s)
* 39 km

The Wildhay River is a fun little river, and the reaches within this report are usually done as a series of day or half-day trips.

"T" Rescue Training — near the group campsite

Classification
1. Overall River: Grade 2
2. Rapids: Class 2 (but can be technical)
3. Skill of Paddlers: Intermediate, or novice under instruction.

Start
The Wildhay River is north of Hinton on Highway #40. After crossing the Wildhay River, continue on to the next intersection (4.1 km), and take the road west towards Rock Lake. Immediately after crossing Moberly creek be sure to take the left turn at the "T." At the next intersection go straight through if going to the Wildhay Group Campsite, or turn right, to continue on to either Rock Lake or the upper former bridge site that is the start of this report. At the next intersection bear left and follow the dirt road to the river and the former bridge site.

Intermediate Access and Distances

Location	km	km	Access &/or Comments
Old Bridge above Group Campsite	0.0		left bank
Old Bridge below Group Campsite	10.0	10.0	left bank
Highway #40 Bridge	15.0	5.0	left bank
above Jarvis Creek	39.0	24.0	right bank

Finish
Access to the finish noted above is via the "Hay River Road." At the north end of W.A. Switzer Park take the "Hay River Road" east and north approximately 12.4 km, and turn left into a meadow and down to the river in approximately 200 m. Just before turning off the Hay River Road you will pass the foundations of an old ranger station, and cross a very small bridge. If you go as far as Jarvis Creek, you have gone too far! **Shuttles** for this run are thus along the Rock Lake Road, highway #40, and the 'Hay River Road.

Gradient
The first section has gradients as high as 6.2 m/km, and much of the lower run reported here drops at 2.6 m/km.

River Volume and Flow Rate
Flows on the Wildhay taper off fairly quickly most years, with the best paddling in June and July. Good paddling can be had at the average flows of 15 to 20 cms. The normal range in early June is from 11 cms to 32 cms, with peak flows of 120 cms reported in June, though other peaks of nearly 100 cms have been reported in July and even in August. No Discharge-Velocity Relationship has been published. The gauging station is just downstream of the group campsite.

Maps
- NTS 1:50.,000: 83 E/9 Moberly Creek, 83 E/8 Rock Lake, 83 F/5 Entrance, and 83 F/12 Gregg lake
(unfortunately the Wildhay flows back and forth across the corner of the first three sheets)
- Provincial Highways Map

Camping
As mentioned, there is a Provincial Forestry Group site on the river just above the first intermediate access point. This site can be booked through the Rock Lake Lodge in Hinton (call 403-865-3295). There are public campsites on Rock Lake upstream and west of these reaches, and at Gregg Lake, off of Highway #40. There is also much "random" camping, particularly at each of the access points, and many good "wilderness" campsites along the river, on all three reaches reported here.

River Notes
This is a fun little river. In my days as an instructor at the Blue Lake Centre I made many, many runs on the first reach here reported — and I've added a good many more since then! Generally the "Hay" is not a powerful or fearsome river, but to avoid the rocks does require good paddling skills.

The first reach is the most interesting. It starts with a little boulder garden, then a gentle kilometer or so, and then a number of tight fast turns. The first left turn leads into a severely undercut cliff. Part way down there are a couple of exposed ledges, the first one on a right turn should be taken well to the inside of the corner. Where ever this river braids out, or forms island, be very watchful for logjams and sweepers. **Do not** enter any channel for which you can not see a safe exit.

The second run from the group site to Highway #40 is often the first run we take new river paddlers down, and the run below Highway #40 (sometimes all the way from camp) makes for a very nice day trip. We have often scared up a herd of elk in the meadows on this run. It too has a couple of interesting chutes, but no really tricky rapids. Again the greatest danger lies in the logjams and sweepers that come and go with each major flood.

As of June '97, the road access to the old bridge site just downstream of the Group Campsite had begun to wash-out. **If** the river breaks through the old road, there will be a few years of dangerous paddling as the river carves a new channel through the trees.

Other Reaches
The Wildhay can be paddled from Rock Lake down; exit Rock Lake on Rock Creek, it soon joins the river. In past years there were some good logjams on this first bit, necessitating a portage! It can make for a fine but long day paddle down to the group campsite. Below Jarvis Creek is two to four days worth of tripping. One further access is available near Pinto Creek. The egress is at the Pine Creek Gas Plant Bridge on the Athabasca (see previous report), and the last dozen or so miles are on the Berland river. It is a long dusty shuttle on the pulp mill haul road on the north side of the Athabasca via Emmerson Lakes.

McLeod River - Mercoal (Highway #40) to McLeod River Recreation Area

Duration of Tour(s)
* 36.7 km
A long day trip or a very nice overnighter, and if you like fishing and walking in picturesque meadows, three days!

Classification
1. Overall River: Grade 2
2. Rapids: Class III
3. Skill of Paddlers: Intermediate paddlers, well experienced with logjams and sweepers.

Start
The start for this run is at the Highway #40 bridge just west of the former locale of Mercoal, south of Hinton on either Highway #40 or the Forestry Trunk Road via Robb.

Finish
The end of this run is in the McLeod River Recreation Area, south of Hinton on the Forestry Trunk Road.   There are a number of access points at and between the new (km 35.4) and old bridges (km 36.7) within the McLeod River Recreation Area. **Shuttles** are driven along highway #40, #47 and the Forestry Trunk Road north of Robb.

Gradient
Gradients on this run vary from 6 m/km to as little as 3.5 m/km, with much of the run between 4.6 to 4.8 m/km.

River Volume and Flow Rate
The following flow volume and rate reports are taken from the hydrology station just above the confluence with the Embarras River. These volumes are approximately double what one should expect at Mercoal. At the Embarras River station normal summer flows range from 10 cms to nearly 70 cms with the greater flows in May and June and considerable drop on average through the month of July. Peak flows in June often exceed 400 cms and some floods have pushed over 900 cms, with one notable flood in early August. Flow rates at this station vary from under 2 km/hr at 25 cms to over 6 km/hr at 400 cms.

Maps
- an up-to-date provincial highways map
- NTS 1:50,000: 83 F/3 Cadomin and 83 F/6 Pedley

Camping
There are a number of public campsites along highways #40 & #47 on the approaches to this run, and the large provincial recreation area at the finish. Once on the river, this is one of those great foothills streams that offers a great campsite at nearly every bend — I do not remember ever having use a poor campsite on this run!

River Notes
This is a fun run. For a couple of years in the '70's we use to race this stretch, in about 3 hours — what a waste! Take more time. The run has lots of gravel chutes and pressure waves, and at various times there have been some complex rapids and ledges in the middle section. One 1 m ledge we called "Froggatt" falls, but in recent years the river has shifted channels and this ledge has been dry. This river does shift, and as a result there are often some pretty tricky, and downright dangerous logjams and sweepers. The run also finishes with a long Class II rapid down to the confluence with the Gregg River, just upstream of the finish.

Other Reaches

The short reach just upstream is a little steeper, smaller, and for some years had a very dangerous logjam near the last railway bridge upstream. The downstream reach to the Embarras River and Highway #47 is a nice three day run, with lots of boulder and small ledge rapids (up to Class III) in the first half. Where the gradient tapers off near highway #16, the washed out trees tend to pile up and there have been some dangerous logjams over the years. Access can be had off of Highway #16 via the Hargwen road, and south of Marlboro, near the cemetery and through an old gravel pit.

Brazeau River - Above Forestry Trunk Road to Reservoir

Duration of Tour(s)
* 110.6 km
- a wonderful long weekend tour for the FTR to Brazeau Reservoir reach, plus some half-day and full day long runs.

Classification
1. Overall River:	Grade 2
2. Rapids:	Class III
3. Skill of Paddlers:	Strong experienced paddlers with good river skills, open canoe paddlers must be able to back paddle and set (back ferry) in fast water. The short run upstream of the FTR can be done by less experienced paddlers

A Brazeau Canyon rest stop!

Start
Access to the upper portion of this report is south off the Cardinal River Road. Go west of the Forestry Trunk Road, and approximately 6.5 km west of the Cardinal River Bridge, turn south and follow the old road to the river bank. This road has been deteriorating and the hill down to the river and ford may require a carry for 300 m.

Intermediate Access and Distances

Location	km	km	Access &/or Comments
Ford above FTR off Cardinal Rd.	0.0		left bank
Forestry Trunk Road (#940 / FTR)	9.3	9.3	right bank, at campground / bridge
Cutline to lower Blackstone Rd.*	39.6	30.3	right bank
Confluence with Blackstone	58.7		right bank / no access
Campground - Brazeau Reservoir	110.6	71.0	along Dam, east side of reservoir

* The middle access, below the canyon and most of the whitewater , is reached by taking the Blackstone Road. This road leaves the Forestry Trunk Road 1.1 km south of the Blackstone Bridge, and heads northeast. Stay left at all intersections. 1.2 km past the gas plant access road you again cross the Blackstone river. 800 m beyond the bridge stay left, then after another 1.8 km stay right. Follow this road for another 5.8 km. After you drop down a hill and cross a creek, you soon pass a well site/gas works on the right. Continue on and through the old gravel pit and follow the trail and cutline to the river. I strongly encourage you to buy the 1:50,000 *Resource Access Map* and find the takeout before commencing, **flag it well!** Do not send some unwary novice down to pick you up! This takeout can require up to a 1 km portage depending on your vehicle and the condition of the trail and cutline.

Finish
Use Secondary Highway #620 south-west from Drayton Valley, past Lodgepole, and then onto the Brazeau Reservoir and Dam. It is well signed. In recent years the upgrading of the Elk River road has been completed and it makes for the shortest, but dustiest shuttle for the big run. The Elk River Road joins the FTR approximately 8 km north of the Brazeau River. **Shuttles** are completed along the Cardinal river road for the upper reach, the FTR and Blackstone road for the middle reach, and along the FTR and Elk River Road (north of the Brazeau) for the long lower reach.

Gradient

The gradient on these reaches varies from 1.2 m/km to a high of 9.5 m/km. The Ford to FTR reach varies from 5.3 m/km to 3.6 m/km. The highest gradient is reached in the second half of the canyon with average gradients between contour lines of 8.0, 9.5, 3.1 and 8.0 m/km. Much of the run below the Canyon drops at gradients between 2.6 and 5.3 m/km. This is one of the runs where I suspect the accuracy of the contour lines at river level and believe that the extreme gradients do average out a little.

River Volume and Flow Rate

The hydrology station for this report is on the first bend below the FTR bridge. Normal flows in June and July vary from approximately 50 cms to 125 cms. The peak flow reported by Alberta Environment exceeds 550 cms and high water generally occurs in June or July, with a rapid drop in flows occurring through August.

Maps

NTS 1:50,000: 83 B/13 Nordegg River, 83 C/15 Cardinal River and 83 C/16 Blackstone River
- an up-to-date Provincial Highways Map
- Alberta Government 1:50,000 *Resource Access Maps* 83 B/13, 83 C/15, and 83 C/16

Camping

Public Campgrounds are available at the FTR bridge and on the Reservoir. There are wonderful wilderness camping sites all along these reaches, both in the canyon and on the flats below.

River Notes

This reach of the Brazeau may be done in three sections. The Ford to the FTR makes for a nice warm-up run and involves mostly rapids formed by gravel chutes and fast corners. The run through the canyon from the FTR to the access of the lower Blackstone road involves much white water and rapids that are strong Class III at most water levels. The white water starts on the second corner below the bridge and just keeps getting better as one descends into the canyon. Approximately 6 km below the bridge there is a complex of two ledges that recently have been easier than some years ago. But, in August '95, the next right bend presented the steepest ledge and chute combination ever remembered on the river. After a brief respite, the long-fun rapids begin through the high gradient sections down to the end of the canyon. From the canyon to the reservoir the river is pretty steady, with just a couple of short lower gradient sections. There are even some fun, easy Class II rapids just upstream of the reservoir. The reservoir can be as much as 13 km of flatwater.

I have paddled this reach many times, and in '95 after two summers of long periods of high water, I found most of the rapids to have been well scoured of gravel, to be much steeper than remembered, and the waves even bigger and stronger than most of my best lies. Rivers do change! After the pleasures of the canyon we were ready to relax on the flats down to the reservoir. But, all that high water had brought down many new trees, and there were many dangerous logjams that required precise maneuvering, and a very watchful eye downstream. I suspect that at some times, many of the braided channels could have been completely obstructed.

Other Reaches

The Brazeau is one stream that I can claim to have paddled from very near its source, all the way to its confluence with a larger stream. A few of us hardy souls have portaged in from the Icefields Parkway, and over Nigel Pass to "bag" this river. There are numerous waterfalls, one great gorge, and many good rapids to be portaged or challenged; and very spectacular scenery to be enjoyed. There is also a run that is frequently tackled above the Ford, starting from either near "Smallboy's" encampment, or the old airfield. This run includes a number of good Class III to IV rapids. One year I took a group of University students down the canal below the reservoir, portaged the powerhouse and second dam, and then ran the river down to the North Saskatchewan and then on to Genessee. This lower run can require that one await the opening of the powerhouse, or be prepared to hike and drag!

Maligne Lake - in Jasper National Park

Introduction

Maligne Lake is one of those spectacular spots one goes to paddle just for the scenery I have twice now taken advantage of the fine campsite that the National Parks service maintains in Samson Narrows, two-thirds of the way down the lake. The mountains around Maligne Lake are spectacular; there is trout fishing in the lake, wildlife is abundant and the camping is good. On the negative side you must share this lake: fortunately only the wardens and the commercial tour operator are allowed power boats, and the commercial tours only go as far south as Spirit Island in the narrows. The best part of the lake for scenery and camping is in the southern third!

Spirit Island — looking into southern 1/3 of the lake

Duration of Tour(s)

From a few hours, to four days. Under good conditions Fisherman's Bay is a three hour paddle, and Coronet Creek is another good two hours beyond the narrows. There is a hiking trail out of Coronet Creek up towards the glacier and another campsite about 6 km to the south. There are also many pleasant short walks and scrambles along the creeks, and avalanche paths flowing into the lake.

Classification

Lake, with the risk of strong winds. The parks service reports that the wind is often out of the south on the north two-thirds of lake, and out of the north on the southern third. Try to plan your paddling for the early morning.

Start & Finish

Maligne Lake is a forty minute drive east and south from the Jasper townsite. Launch your own boat at the Maligne Lake public boat launch on the NW corner of the lake, or charter from the boat rental concession on the NE corner of the lake. You must drive pass Maligne Lake Lodge, and cross the Maligne river to reach the public boat launch.

Distance Summary

Distances have been calculated from the 1:50,000 N.T.S. sheets, and were plotted by roughly following the east shore north of the narrows and the west shore south of the narrows. These distances should provide the shortest shoreline route, but may put you in conflict with the reported winds. Opposite shore distances should only be slightly longer. A mid-lake line is about 1 km shorter for the whole lake.

Location	km	km	Access &/or Comments
Public Boat Launch, N.W. Corner	0.0		
Leah Creek	5.3	5.3	Picnic Site
Fisherman's Bay Campsite	13.3	8.0	floating dock, deep in the bay
Spirit Island dock	14.7	1.4	short walking/interpretative trail
Spindly Creek	17.3	2.6	Picnic Site
Coronet Creek Campsite	22.4	5.1	on the east side of the delta
Creek fan, SE end of the lake	23.2	0.8	

Maps

- N.T.S. 1:50,000: *83 C/12 Athabasca Falls & 83 C/11 Southesk Lake*
- Map Town Publishing 1:100,000; *Jasper & Maligne Lake*, Calgary, Alberta, 1994 (my first choice)

Camping

National Park Service:
- Fisherman's Bay off the NE corner of Samson Narrows, eight tent pads.
- Coronet Creek at the South end of the lake, eight tent pads.

Each of these sites includes picnic tables, fire rings (gather drift wood along the lake shore away from the campsite) and bear-proof food storage cabinets. No unorganised camping is allowed. Many good park service campgrounds exist in the Jasper townsite area for pre and post trip camping.

Beware, the parks service has some restrictions on the campsites (as of 1996), campers are limited to only four nights on the lake, two each, at Fisherman's Bay in the narrows, and Coronet Creek at the south end. Group size is limited to six, and each campsite has only eight tent pads. Campsite permits are required, and reservations are accepted (for an additional fee!) and recommended. To book call the Jasper Trail Office at 403-852-6177, other Park Information is at 403-852-6161.

Tour Notes:

Maligne Lake is the longest lake, and third deepest lake in the Canadian Rockies. Maligne Lake would appear to have been infrequently visited by the native and metis hunters in the late 19th century. The first reported European visitor would appear to have been the railroad surveyor, Henry Mcleod, who in 1875 called it "Sorefoot Lake." In 1908, Mary Schäffer, with guides Bill Warren and Sidney Unwin, using directions provided by the Stoney Indian, Samson Beaver, "rediscovered" Maligne Lake. Mary Schäffer revisited and mapped the lake for the Canadian Government in 1911, and later published a book, *Old Indian Trails of the Canadian Rockies* that did much to provide early publicity of the beauties of the lake. This book has been reprinted as *A Hunter of the Peace*. Over my years on and around Maligne Lake, Lois and I have had the pleasure viewing wildlife ranging from Osprey and Loons to Slate Colored Juncos, Woodland Caribou to Thirteen Lined Chipmunks, and on our last venture we just missed a morning black bear encounter. Our early rising campground neighbors told us with some "relish" of just how close the bear had been to our tent! Paddlers should be prepared for bear encounters. Fishermen will require a National Park License, those under 16 years fish on an accompanying adult's license.

Jarvis Lake and Creek - in William A. Switzer Park

Duration of Tour
* 6+ km one way

Jarvis Lake and Creek can make for a pleasant day paddle for experienced paddlers with young families or for a youth group, or it can be a great little training run for new paddlers. Good paddlers can make the round trip in an afternoon, new paddlers should pack a lunch!

Jarvis Lake — near Kelly's Bathtub

Classification
1. Overall River: Grade 1
2. Rapids: Class 1
3. Skill of Paddlers: Beginner, should be able to turn the canoe and keep it running straight.

Start / Finish
This trip can be started at either end, especially if making it a round trip. The creek does flow from Jarvis Lake to Cache Lake. The Jarvis Lake picnic site is reached by taking the south W.A. Switzer Park access road off of Highway #40. Cache Lake is accessed from the highway via the campground road into the Beaver Ranch, Graveyard and Cache Lake campsites.

Intermediate Access and Distances
Distance measurement was started at the Jarvis Lake Picnic site at the south end of Jarvis Lake. Highway #40 crosses the creek at km 3.6 and a side trip can be made into Kelly's Bathtub (a little kettle pond) at the north end of Jarvis Lake (km 3.2) The Blue Lake Centre is on Blue Lake at approximately km 4.3. These distances were calculated from a 1:50,000 sheet and are all approximations! Cache Lake campsite is somewhat over 6 km from the Jarvis Lake picnic site, and about 200 m down the creek from Cache Lake.

Gradient
The biggest gradients on this run are the occasional beaver dams that needs to be "run" or pushed over, or worse, drug up on the upstream paddle.

River Volume and Flow Rate
Not much! This run is best paddled in years when the beavers have done some flooding; if all the dams are out it can be a bit of a "muddy drag."

Maps
- NTS 1:50,000 83 F/5 Entrance

Camping
The nicest, and most private campsites (primitive facilities though) have been those at Cache and Graveyard lake. A more modern campsite with better facilities is just to the north at Gregg Lake. There is also a group campsite at Pine Bay on the west side of Jarvis Lake. For reservation information for Gregg Lake, or to book the Pine Bay Group site call the Hinton Forest Office at 403-865-5600.

Lake / River Notes

Jarvis Lake is approximately 3 km long but never more than a few hundred meters wide. It is deep in the valley and generally well sheltered. With the creek it is a great place to learn how to paddle! One can get wet on the creek, clambering out, pushing, shoving, sliding in off the beaver dams! It can be great fun on a hot day. And the "jack" fishing can be good!

Edson to Lake Wabamun region — rivers and lakes

McLeod River -- Highway #47 to Whitecourt

Duration of Tour(s)
* 206 km
- from ½ day to multi-day tours.

Classification
1. Overall River: Grade 1
2. Rapids: Class I - II
3. Skill of Paddlers: Practised Novice with basic river skills.

Start
Highway #47 (the Coal Branch) Bridge just above the confluence with the
Embarras River, south and west of Edson.

Intermediate Access and Distances

Ceyana kids in a side canyon

Location	km	km	Access &/or Comments
Highway #47 - Embarras River	0.0		
Hudson's Bay Gas Plant Bridge	25.0	25.0	left bank
Wilmore Recreation Park - Edson	37.5	12.5	left bank
South of Edson - Golf Course Road	40.5	3.0	left bank
Moose Creek Rapids & Island	43.6		no access
Highway #16 bridge	53.5	13.0	poor access
Highway #16A bridge	58.8	5.3	right bank
Rosevear Ferry	84.0	25.2	either bank - beware of cables
Old Peers Bridge site	100.8	16.8	
Highway #32 (Peers) Bridge	102.5	1.7	left bank
Access South of Goat Creek	177.0	74.5	left bank
Whitecourt - #43 Bridge	204.4	27.4	
Whitecourt - Athabasca River	206.0	1.6	left bank

Finish
The finish for this run is the boat access on the last few yards of the left bank before the confluence with the
Athabasca. To reach this boat launch turn east off of Highway #43 just south of the Athabasca River bridge.
Shuttles for this run may be driven along and off of Highways #47, #16, #748, and #32.

Gradient
The gradients for this run vary from 2.5 to .7 m/km, with many of the average gradients between contour
intervals varying little from 1 m/km.

River Volume and Flow Rate

At the hydrology station just upstream of the start of this run, the normal flows in May, June and early July vary from 20 cms to nearly 70 cms, with some peak flows exceeding 1000 cms. Most peak flows have been recorded at this station in June and early July, with at least one major flood in early August. Velocities at this station vary from just 2 km/hr at 25 cms to 4 km/hr at 100 cms and 6 km/hr at 300 cms.

At the Whitecourt station normal flows for May through late July range from 25 cms to 160 cms. Peak floods at Whitecourt have approached 1800 cms! At the Whitecourt station velocities range from just over 2 km/hr at 80 cms to 6 km/hr at 500 cms.

Maps

- NTS 1:50,000: 83 F/7 Erith, 83 F/10 Bickerdike, 83 F/9 Edson. 83 G/12 Carrot Creek, 83 G/13 Hattonford, and 83 J/4 Whitecourt
- an up-to-date Provincial Highways Map

Camping

A public campground is available on the river at Wilmore Park near Edson. Campgrounds within a few miles of the river occur at Bear Lake north of the Rosevear Ferry, near the Peers Bridges, at Goat Creek on Highway #32 and in Whitecourt. Wilderness camping is available along much of the Mcleod. This statement must be tempered with the fact that much of the run is through farmland, and some sections are rather muskegie. On most days one must start their campsite search early and often take a "not perfect -- make do" site. If you find a secluded "ideal" site early — take it! The next one may be a long way down the river.

River Notes

As one may suspect from the gradient reports above, the McLeod on these reaches is not a fast flowing, furious, white water stream. This is a pleasant run, that is occasionally interrupted with brief riffles. Although, at most water levels there may still be the occasional sweeper and logjam to be avoided.

The first hazard may be still the old bridge piers that appear at some water levels just below the put-in. They may even require scouting at some water levels. They are usually runable without problem! Another sometime problem, at higher water levels, can be at "Big Eddy" at the confluence with Sundance Creek. This is usually just a very fine and popular fishing hole, but at high water can demonstrate interesting hydrological dynamics.

Possibly the most complex rapid and one that novices should certainly stop to scout would be the Moose Creek rapids, at km 43.6. These rapids start at the head of the island, and continue along the right bank all the way to Moose Creek at the left bend below the island. At most flows paddlers take the excitement on the right side of the Island, and at higher flows you may be able to sneak along the left channel. Some paddlers have even been known to portage through the farmyard on the left bank. One memorable group even borrowed the farmer's tractor, without permission. Paddlers were not popular with this farmer for some years — maybe even still so!

In 1991 I lead a "very fine-time-had-by-all," long weekend, Ceyana trip on the Peers to Goat Creek section. We remember the run as an easy paddle where the older kids had an early chance to command their own boats. In addition we camped in a small canyon, the second night out on a creek fan (km 156.7). The creek had cut the side canyon pictured above. And, just before our departure from this site, our new elkhound, Thor, had his first successful bear encounter — he put the run on the bear! About half-way along on this last day, we encountered some very nice riffles and waves in a shallow canyon at kms 162 to 164. We pulled out, as many do, just above Goat Creek. Most reports of the last few miles into Whitecourt indicate that the river tends to be broad, shallow and very slow going.

Lobstick River - from Highway #22 to the Pembina River

adapted from a report submitted by Ted Bentley

Duration of Tour
* 13.2 km
From a day to less than a half-day.

Classification

Lois and Nick Lees in the rapid above the Evansburg bridge

1. Overall River   Grade 2
2. Rapids   Class I to II - Class III in very high water.
3. Skill of Paddler   Intermediate, or novice accompanied by a skilled guide/instructor.

Start
Follow Hwy #16 west of Edmonton about 110 km, turn north on Hwy. #22, 3 km west of Evansburg, travel 1.5 km north, best access to water is from the north bank, east side of the bridge.

Intermediate Access & Distances
1) Range Road #81, North bank, reached by traveling 2 mi. north, 2 mi. west, and ½ mi. south from Evansburg. This access requires a 1/4 mile portage down a rough road allowance.
     - 7.1 km from finish.
2) Evansburg Bridge, right/south bank on the west side of the road, 2 km north of Hwy #16.
     - 1.3 km from finish.

Finish
In the Pembina Provincial Park, Pembina River beach across from the confluence of the Lobstick and Pembina Rivers. Reached from the lowest loop road in the camping area of the park. **Shuttles** are best driven along Hwy. #16a.

Gradient
The greatest gradient on the upper section is 7.2 m/km, with an overall average of approximately 4 m/km.

River Volume and Flow Rate
The hydrology station for the Lobstick is right at the Highway #22 bridge. The highest average flows occur in late April and early May, with the normal range reported as between 4 and 12 cms. Some peak discharges have approached 100 cms, in late June and July! No Discharge/Velocity data have been published.

Maps
- NTS 1:50,000: 83 G/11 Chip Lake, 83 G/10 Isle Lake (barely touched - last 200 m)

Camping
A great public campground is available at Pembina River Park, across from the mouth of the Lobstick. There are individual campsites almost on the river bank, and a great group camping area that can be reserved (call Wabamun Provincial Park at 403-892-2702).

River Notes

This trip is best between April and June when the water is high. Late in the year water levels may be too low to float boats. The Lobstick is a narrow river that puts the paddler in intimate contact with its surrounding environment. From the Hwy. 22 bridge, the river gradually descends into scenic Paskapoo sandstone banks. The sandstone formations provide the variety of ledges and rock gardens which make the paddling excellent white water practice for novices and beginners in the company of a competent coach or instructor. The deeply muskeg-colored water combined with the brown sandstone can make it difficult to see the boulders in slow current areas and you need to watch carefully to avoid running on to them. The water is usually shallow and almost always allows a dumped paddler to walk to shore.

From Hwy. 22 to Rng. Rd. 81 there is first a very placid few kilometers, then some rock gardens and an interesting ledge that is usually Class 2 but can become Class 3 in high water. From Rng. Rd. 81 to the Evansburg Bridge there is a series of placid sections interspersed with features that are never more than Class 2 but provide all the types of features found on other white water. This section of 6.7 km is just excellent for introducing people to playing with white water. Most first time paddlers can manage to recirculate through these features without being intimidated. From the Evansburg Bridge to the Provincial Park is a continuous 1.3 km Class 2 rock garden that goes to Class 3 in very high water. The whole of the Lobstick is excellent practice in reading water and maneuvering a boat. At low water the Lobstick can be a very discouraging and tedious paddle because of all the rocks.

Natural / Cultural History Notes

As mentioned above, the valley of the Lobstick is cut down into the Paskapoo Geological Formation. Coal seams as well as the softly shaped sandstone beds provide some fairly steep banks. These can be unstable after prolonged rain or during spring thaw and will drop medium and large blocks into the water. Although there are usually steep banks on one side, access to land from the water is usually very easy on the other side.

There is quite a bit of petrified wood with some coal inclusions on the stream bed. Two thirds of the way between the Evansburg Bridge and the park, there is a high bank on the left side that has some poorly fossilized clams in the formation. They are probably a recent fresh water species. Iron concretions, rust brown fine grained rocks, are also very common on the stream bed. The ecosystem in the area is mixed aspen and spruce. Moose, deer and very occasionally bears are sighted. Water foul includes blue heron, mergansers, and goldeye. In very low water years beavers may dam the whole river late in the season.

The original trail to Jasper, the Foley Trail, crossed the Pembina in the area of the provincial Park and followed along the north bank of the Lobstick to about the Hwy 22 Bridge. Homesteaders moved into the area about 1905 and over time when the railway bridge across the Pembina near the present Hwy 16 was built. Gradually the main transportation route moved a couple of miles south of the Lobstick but still paralleled it.

Pembina River - Raven Creek Road Bridge to Sangudo

Duration of Tour(s)
* 322.8 km
This report includes a number of day and multi-day tours.

Classification

The Pembina Princesses

1. Overall River: Grade 1 for Lodgepole to Easyford, and Pembina River Provincial Park to Sangudo Grade 2 for the upper reach and the 56 km above Pembina River Provincial Park.

2. Rapids: Class I to II, possibly Class III at high water on Grade 2 reaches

3. Skill of Paddlers: Novice with basic strokes and river skills for the Grade 1
For the Grade 2 reaches greater skill is required -- a good knowledge of basic strokes and river maneuvers is required, rock dodging abilities are important, and the occasional sweeper and log jam must be avoided. This is a great little river for open canoe paddlers!

Start
The Raven Creek Road bridge is southwest of Wolf Lake and may be accessed from the north via the Conoco - Peco Gas Plant. For our 1994 trip we met in Lodgepole, then drove out to the Wolf Lake Road bridge, dropped off a shuttle vehicle and then proceeded north past Wolf Lake and up to the Peco Gas Plant road junction, then back west and south to the bridge -- up-to-date maps are most necessary!!

Intermediate Access and Distances

Location	km	km	Access &/or Comments
Raven Creek Road Bridge	0.0		either bank
Wolf Lake Road Bridge	37.6	37.6	either bank
Road access South of Zeta Lake	57.8	20.2	left bank
Hwy. #753 Bridge N. of Lodgepole	113.3	55.5	left bank
Hwy. #621 Bridge W. of Easyford	153.8	40.5	right bank
Rd. Access @ PK 263210 (UMG)	194.5	40.7	right bank
Rd. Access @ PK 307251 (UMG)*	214.5	20.0	left bank, near small creek
Pembina River Park - Day Use	250.8	36.3	right bank
Lobstick River confluence	251.9	1.1	left / no access
Pembina River Park - Campground	252.0	0.1	right bank
Matthews Crossing	267.8	15.8	right bank / 300 m portage required
Rangeton Community Park	293.0	25.2	left bank
Sangudo	322.8	29.8	right bank

* PK 307251 is reached by turning south at Evansburg, first turn west of the bridge, and following Rge.Rd. #80 due south to the river.

Finish

The finish for this run is next to the fair grounds and campground in Sangudo, just off of Highway #43 and through the town.

Gradient

The upper reach below the Raven Creek Road Bridge mostly varies between 3 to 4 m/km. There is one stretch in the middle, starting above the pipeline crossing (km 19) that calculates at 8.5 m/km., then a 1.7 m/km, and a 6.6 m/km. Our experience was that the worst rapids were just below the pipeline crossing in the lowest gradient stretch! Contour lines do lie at times!!

The run between the Wolf Lake Road Bridge and the next access is consistently between 2.8 and 3.8 m/km. Then the run down to Lodgepole varies between 1.5 and 2.8 m/km. Between Lodgepole and Sangudo, only the last hour above Pembina River Park exceeds 2 m/km, and actually calculates at 2.8 m/km.

Flow Rate and River Volume

During the summer months of June and July the river volume averages approximately 25 CMS, with a normal range (25 to 75 percentile) of approximately 10 CMS to 80 CMS. The extreme range of volumes reported between 1956 and 1985 is from less than 10 CMS to more than 700 CMS for June and July at Pembina River Park. Weekly average volumes, and the range of volumes reported, is less during the spring, late summer and fall months.

The rate of stream flow varies with volume, from less than 2 kmph with 20 CMS to 7 kmph with more than 500 cms. This data is for the hydrology station just below the Highway 16a Bridge, in Pembina River Park.

Maps

 - an up-to-date Provincial Highways Map
 - the following NTS 1:50,000 sheets:

Raven Creek 83 F/1	Zeta Lake 83 G/4
Blue Rapids 83 G/3	Easyford 83 G/6
Tomahawk 83 G/7	Isle Lake 83 G/10
Chip Lake 83 G/11	Sangudo 83 G/15

Camping

Public campgrounds are available on the river at the Pembina River Provincial Park, Easyford, Rangeton and Sangudo Municipal Park. The group site at the Pembina River Provincial Park is wonderful (book through Wabamun Provincial Park at 403-892-2702)! It provides a great base for a canoe club, outdoor ed. class or scout troop. It also provides good access for the early spring white water on the Lobstick river.

Random camping is generally available along most of the river reaches contained in this report, but below Highway #16 much of the camping is along farmland, and the private property owners must be respected. The upper reaches are within the Forest Zone, and the reach above Highway #16a has much camping on the river beaches below the high water mark.

River Notes

This report really covers a variety of reaches. The upper reaches and the reach above the Provincial Park really do require good river skills. The Lodgepole, Easyford and lower reaches can be safely paddled at most lower water levels by relatively inexperienced paddlers under the guidance of a good coach.

The reach above the Wolf Lake road has only recently been paddled by members of the Ceyana Club for the first time (an overnight trip!). We paddled it with the river flowing with approximately 45 CMS at Entwistle. Many rock gardens were present, and surprisingly very few log jams. A particularly notable rock garden, that ran on for about 250 m, was found just below the pipeline crossing at UMG reference NJ 574912.

At present I have not paddled the section from the Wolf Lake Road to Easyford, but others have reported no serious problems, and the map would lead one to believe that the most serious difficulties may be logjams and sweepers in the reach south of Zeta Lake, and upstream of Lodgepole.

The run from Easyford to Pembina River we once did as a four day canoe trip. The first section is quite flat, and then there were some fun Class II rapids. At UMG PK 303235, the river makes a very sharp left bend, and the river is cutting the corner and has formed a number of channels and logjams — it can be tight, or was when we were there.

A favorite run of the canoe club is the 36 km above Pembina River Provincial Park. In past years we often did this as a long day run of 6 - 7 hours, and once, in just over 3 hours at high water. The past couple of trips though have been as overnight trips, which have allowed for an easy Saturday start from Edmonton, and an early arrival home on Sunday. This is a favorite run, as the river starts easy, gathers momentum and provides the best white water in the last hour to the finish.

In June, 1992, we had a wonderful relaxing trip on the reach from Pembina River Park to the Rangeton Community Park. We spent one night on the river and all the kids had a chance to manage their own craft. The water was running at only 11 CMS! Some rock gardens we had to walk!

The Pembina has a good reputation for hiding boat grabbing boulders. The muskeg colored, brown-tinged water nicely hides the brown Pembina Formation sandstones that predominate.

The Pembina has always provided a good range of wildlife viewing ranging from deer, elk and moose, to hawks, eagles and ospreys. Even the fishing has been good on some trips!

Wabamun Lake - North Shore

Duration of Tour(s)
* 25.2 km

Wabamun Lake lends itself to both part and full day trips. The developed nature of the lakeshore precludes any sort of a wilderness camping experience.

Classification
Wabamun is a flatwater, lake paddle, requiring only basic canoe skills. Wabamun is a big lake and subject to summer squalls and storms — paddlers should remain close to shore!

Start
Wabamun Lake Provincial Park is approximately a 45 minute drive west of Edmonton on Highway #16. The Park is south of the Highway on the very northeast corner of the Lake; watch for the signs along Highway #16.

Intermediate Access and Distances - along the north shore

Location	km	km	Access &/or Comments
Wabamun Prov. Park pier	0.0		
Railway Trestle - Moonlight Bay	1.0	1.0	
town of Wabamun Pier	2.2	1.2	
Point Alison - end of	3.3	1.1	
Camp Ernest Poole - Scouts Canada	12.5	9.2	
road access east of Fallis - Coal Point	15.1	2.6	
YWCA Camp YoWoChAs	15.3	0.2	
Coal Point - end of	16.3	1.0	
road access south of Fallis-Coal Point	17.5	1.2	
Seba Beach -Yacht Club	24.4	6.9	
Seba Beach - Main Pier	25.2	0.8	

Finish
Seba Beach is approximately a 60 minute drive east of Edmonton on Highway #16, and is south of the Highway on Secondary Highway #759.

Maps
- an up-to-date Provincial Highways Map
- N.T.S. 1:250,000: 83 G Wabamun Lake
- N.T.S. 1:50,000: 83 G/9 Onoway, and 83 G/10 Isle Lake

Camping
A large Provincial Parks campground is available at Wabamun Lake Provincial Park on Moonlight Bay Within the park there are two group camp sites, one with a camp kitchen and the second has a large open field and is the one closer to the lake. There is also a day-use group site available for private or youth group bookings (403-892-2702). There is a large privately run campground/resort on the west side of Seba Beach, but it is not right on the lake.

Lake Notes

Wabamun Lake is one of the larger lakes in the Edmonton Area. Wabamun, like all larger bodies of open water on the prairies, is subject to sudden winds and the development of large steep waves. Much of the north shore has been developed for cottages. Possibly the best wildlife viewing may be the NW shore of Moonlight Bay within the provincial park, and from Coal Point to Seba Beach (this stretch of the lake has no immediate road access!). The older power plant near the town of Wabamun still uses lake water directly for cooling, and consequently the NE end of Wabamun is often the first open water in the area for spring paddling. In fact, local white water paddlers train on the cooling canals most of the winter and often have their gates hung just west of the town site. The east and southeast shores of the lake are within the Wabamun Indian Reserve 133A.

Sundre, Red Deer, Drumheller and Rocky Mountain House - rivers

Red Deer River - Big Horn Creek in the Ya Ha Tinda to below Coal Camp

Duration of Tour(s)
* 76.2 km
- from three days to a couple of hours, with many wonderful slow half-day paddles -- to allow for all the "play" spots to be properly utilized!

Classification
1. Overall River: Grade 2
2. Rapids: Class I to IV
3. Skill of Paddlers: From practised novice with good leadership in group, or intermediate paddlers with good river skills.

J. Faulkner Family — above Bighorn Creek

Start
Bighorn Creek is accessed by heading west at the junction just on the north side of the Forestry Trunk Road bridge over the Red Deer. It is almost an one hour drive to Bighorn Creek, if the road is rough or wet. Bighorn Creek to Mountainaire Lodge is generally considered to be a long days paddle. Many of the intermediate access points listed below provide excellent starting points for shorter paddles.

This whole area is usually reached via Highway #2 to Olds, west on #27 to Sundre, then west on #584 for 8 km, then turn left -- note the Mountainaire Lodge signs -- follow them! Stay on the "main road."

Distances, Intermediate Access, Gradient and Difficulty Summary

Location/Elevation/Class	Running Mileage (km)	Intermediate Distances (km)	Average Gradients (m/km)	Comments
Bighorn Creek	0			left bank
5100'	1.9		4.3	Logjams and sweepers on this run
5000'	8.9		4.4	to Wildhorse Meadows.
4900'	15.7		7.9	
start - Wildhorse Creek Meadow	18.3			left bank, steep climb
4800'	19.5		7.1	
Wildhorse Creek ledge (II)	20.0			
Wildhorse Creek Access	20.2	20.2		left bank, rough road
Wildhorse Creek	21.2			left side, no access
Panther River ledges (II - III)	23.1			novice paddlers should scout!
Panther River	23.3			right side, no access
4700'	23.7		5	

Location/Elevation/Class	Running Mileage (km)	Intermediate Distances (km)	Average Gradients (m/km)	Comments
FTR Bridge / Mountainaire Lodge	26.1	5.9		right or left bank
Fisher Creek ledges (II - III)	27.4			
Fisher Creek	27.9			group campsite 200 m up the creek
River Access	28.1			right bank
Yara Creek	29.1			left side, no access
Airfield / river access	29.5	3.4		left bank
4600'	29.7		5.8	
Big Rock rapid (III)	30.1			scout or portage on left
Gas Plant access	31.8			left bank, short walk
small ledge	32.1			scout or portage on left bank - is changing, channel is shifting north ('97)
upper Gooseberry rapid (III - IV)	33.9			scout right bank, portage left bank
Gooseberry ledge	34.1			portage on left bank
Jimbo's Staircase (III - IV)	34.4			scout or portage on left bank
4500'	34.9		7	
"S" Bend rapid (II - III)	35.5			access on left bank, short walk
Pipeline Crossing	37.1	7.6		left bank
Nationals Site rapid (III - IV)	37.3			scout or portage on either bank
4400'	39.2		4.1	
Wysenchuk's Crossing	42.1	5		left bank
Burnt Timber Creek	42.8			right side
Sauna Hole rapid (II - III)	44.1			
4300'	46.6		5.3	
Diagonal Ledge	47.8			
Upper Cache Hill ledges (III - IV)	48.0			scout first drop from left, last drop on right, (last ledge has diminished as of '97).
Cache Hill rapid (II - III)	48.8			scout from left bank
Cache Hill Access & lower ledge (II - III)	49.4	7.3		access on left bank, two channels, scout from both shores.
4200'	52.2		7.6	Some very good gravel chutes &
4150'	54.2		4.3	small ledges on this run.
Williams Creek Rapid (II - III)	57.1			

Location/Elevation/Class	Running Mileage (km)	Intermediate Distances (km)	Average Gradients (m/km)	Comments
Williams Creek	57.3			left side, no access
4100'	57.9		5.7	
4050'	60.6		6.9	
Access from Road	60.8			left bank
4000'	62.8		5.2	
Double Ledge (III - IV, often very powerful)	63.3	13.9		access on left bank, steep path scout or portage from either shore.
Cartier Creek	65.3			This stretch is often referred to as
3950'	65.7		3.9	the "mad mile", a great teaching run!
Coal Camp ledge & access	66.4	3.1		access on left bank, be sure to scout drop if unfamiliar!
Funkhauser rapid (II)	69.0			
3900'	69.6		3.9	Some good, strong gravel chutes
3850'	72.0		6.4	on this run. Also logjams and
3800'	74.8		5.5	sweepers to be avoided!
road access @ umg PH 532369	76.2	9.8		left bank, short dirt road to pavement

* not all rapids have been noted!

* conditions change with volume and from year to year!

* single drop ledges are hard to classify, if in doubt -- SCOUT!

Finish

The last run reported here finishes approximately 12 km west and south of Sundre. Approximately three kilometers south of the turn off from #584, take the dirt road off the pavement and follow the section line south, approximately 400 m down to the river. **Shuttles** are all driven along the road that parallels the river.

Gradient

Gradients on these reaches of the Red Deer vary from a low of 3.9 m/km to a high of 7.9 m/km. All reaches have some high gradient stretches, but rapid difficulty is really dictated by geology.

River Volume and Flow Rate

The hydrology station is listed as "below the mouth of Burnt Timber Creek". It is, well below, much closer to "Cache Hill." In June and July, flow may vary from less than 25 cms to more than 300 cms, with normal flow (the 25 to 75 percentile) ranging from approximately 30 cms to 78 cms. Once over about 100 cms this river becomes significantly more dangerous.

No velocity data has been published for this hydrology station. For all reaches at normal flow levels there are no slow stretches -- river time is dictated by how long your group chooses to "play" each rapid. White water groups on this river tend to take short paddles, and play lots, as almost all the rapids have good eddies that allow one to work back upstream for a "another run."

Maps
- NTS 1:250,000 - 82 O Calgary
- NTS 1:50,000 - 82 O/12 Barrier Mountain, 82 O/11 Burnt Timber Creek, & 82 O/10 Fallen Timber Creek
- an up-to-date highways map

Camping
Provincial Forest Service
- Wildhorse Creek, west of the Forestry Trunk Road
- Yara Creek, near the FTR crossing
- Red Deer River Recreational Area - south of Mountainaire Lodge - 1.5 km
- Fisher Creek Group Campsite - south of Mountainaire Lodge - 2 km (book at 403-932-4725)
- Deer Creek, east of the FTR
- Cartier Creek Recreational Area - near Coal Camp

Unorganized - no facilities and rough road access
- Bighorn Creek (very popular with the "horse set")
- Wildhorse Creek Meadows
- Gooseberry Flats
- Wysenchuck's Crossing
- Cache Hill

Wilderness
- many good sites exist along the river, the biggest problem being closeness to the road, possibly the best reaches to avoid the road are; below Bighorn Creek, below Wysenchuck's crossing, and below Cache Hill.

River Notes
This is Alberta's pre-eminent white water stream. No other river in the province attracts the usage that the Red Deer receives. It is near our population centers, it has excellent access, reliable water all season, great camping, and challenges for everyone. Yet, its moderate volume is generally not threatening. Here is a river leaders and commercial outfitters can safely take relative novices on, a river with a teaching or practise site on every second corner, and yet, enough "solid" water challenges to keep most experienced paddlers interested. This is a river for everyone -- and unfortunately on some summer weekends, everyone comes: rafters, fishermen, hotdoggers, novices, commercial tours, university groups, everyone! Some days it does seem a little crowded -- if possible plan your summer season trips for mid-week and avoid the crowds. If out on a crowed weekend, please share the "play spots" -- take a couple of turns, and then move on.

White water paddling grew up in Alberta, on this stretch of the Red Deer. Our early closed-boat paddlers learned their skills and explored the river for the rest of us in the summer of 1971. In 1972 the Canadian White Water Nationals came west for the first time to the Red Deer. We still refer to that year's slalom site as the "Nationals Site." The national championships returned in 1976. In '72 the wildwater event was held on the lower Panther. By '76 the sport and Alberta paddlers were ready to race on the Red Deer, over the Gooseberry ledge, and down Jimbo's staircase.

Jimbo's Staircase takes its name from our first home grown C-1 paddler. Jim swam, followed his C-1 down the staircase, and suffered no more than the necessity of repairing his boat's bow, and the ignominity of having the rapid named for him.

Popular Reaches and for whom:
- *for novices:* (should have basic control strokes, and have been introduced to basic river maneuvers before heading downstream)
    - F.T.R. to Gas Plant (scout ledges above Fisher Creek, and portage the Big Rock)
    - Cache Hill to above Double Ledge
    - Coal Camp to lower access
- *next runs:*
    - below Double ledge to Coal Camp
    - Wysenchuk Crossing to Cache Hill
    - Bighorn Creek to Forestry Trunk Road
- *most excitement -- better paddlers:*
    - Gas Plant to below Nationals Site

Historical Notes

Ya Ha Tinda and the upper Red Deer were central to the territories of the Stoney Indians, the inhabitants at the time of exploration and settlement by Europeans. These Stoney had not been in the area long, and themselves were recent migrants from the north central plains. Like many later European settlers, they came seeking peace and new hunting lands, away from the warring Sioux. In Ya Ha Tinda, the Kootenay Plains and the Bow valley they found abundant game, large wintering areas that offered good grazing, and warm chinook winds that broke the long cold winters and kept the grasses exposed for their herds of horses. The Stoneys were one of Robert Rundle's first successes for conversion to Christianity. Rundle, a Wesleyan Methodist, and the first Protestant missionary to Alberta, traveled many times through the upper Red Deer region during the 1840's. Unlike many other streams in Alberta, the Red Deer did not support a major canoe route. The Red Deer was generally too shallow, its upper reaches did not break the mountain barrier, and the lower reaches were held by the aggressive Blackfoot tribes. But the Red Deer has proved a fine recreational stream, and paddlers have been reporting tours since the 1930's. The upper Red Deer has supported commercial rafters since the early '70s.

For many years in the late seventies and mid-eighties, open boat paddlers met each fall at Cache Hill for *the Muskeg Cup*, a series of events including: a short slalom, lining and poling, a wildwater race, and even "flour packing." It was a true test for an "all-round" paddlers and outdoors persons. Everyone competed both as one of a mixed pair, and solo. It was a great event for over a decade!

Wildlife Notes

The upper Red Deer valley is home to virtually all of the species of the eastern slopes, including grizzly bears and cougars. Spotting large wildlife from the river is often difficult, and the heavy recreational use of the valley does tend to force large game into the more secluded side valleys. In recent years deer populations have been good, and are often spotted from the canoe, or far more often, on the Friday evening drive in for a weekend of paddling. The river valley supports a wide variety of bird life, and paddlers will often spot osprey, kingfishers, dippers and the occasional eagle.

Other Reaches

In former times we were able to drive to the National Park boundary and this provided another great ½ day paddle. Scalp Creek washed out the bridge a few years ago and we seem to have lost this run -- a mixed blessing. To the best of our knowledge we can find no documented reports of running the Red Deer from its headwaters to the Banff Park boundary. The 1974 guide, *Wild Rivers - Alberta*, suggests that at least the last 16 km of this run are navigable up-stream of the boundary. A map survey would suggest that the stream should be runnable (except for a canyon or two, and couple or three water falls) from Douglas Lake, or Red Deer Lakes. Access is the problem, one may be able to portage in from Lake Louise, and hire a horse outfitter to carry in supplies.

Downstream there is approximately 19 more km of fast, braided water into Sundre. This lower reach is often full of tight, tricky logjams! Beware of the "tank traps" just upstream of Sundre.

Red Deer River - Red Deer to Drumheller

Duration of Tour
* 210 km
* 5 - 6 days
This reach of the Red Deer has many access points that allow a variety of half-day to multi-day trips.

Classification

Overall River -   Grade 1
Rapids -   Class I to easy II
Paddling Skills - Practised novice, with basic skills to ferry, do eddy turns and control canoe direction.

At Dry Island Buffalo Jump

Start

The primary start for this run is within the city of Red Deer, at the boat launch in Great West Park opposite the Water Treatment Plant and just upstream of the old CPR bridge. This boat launch may be reached by taking 59 Street west off Gaetz Avenue (Hwy. #2A), and then south on Kerry Wood Drive. Or by taking the 67 Street Access off of Hwy. #2, then Taylor Drive south, and then east onto Kerry Wood Drive. The boat launch is signed on Kerry Wood Drive.

Intermediate Access and Distances

Location	km	km	Access &/or Comments
Red Deer	0.0		left bank at boat launch
Burbank - county park	21.2	21.2	left bank, below Blindman River, watch for the stairs
Joffre Bridge Hwy #815	39.8	18.6	right bank, below bridge
Content Bridge Hwy #21	88.8	49.0	left bank, above bridge
Trenville Park	118.0	29.2	right bank, just below the island
Mckenzie Crossing Hwy #590	125.6	7.6	left bank, below bridge
Dry Island Buffalo Jump	139.7	14.1	right bank
Tolman Bridge Hwy #585	154.9	15.2	either bank, below bridge
Morin Bridge Hwy #27	178.9	24.0	left bank, 1 km above bridge, or 100 m below the bridge
Bleriot Ferry	188.4	9.5	right bank, .4 km below ferry crossing in campsite
Drumheller	210.0	21.6	right bank, below Hwy. #9 bridge

Finish
The finish for this run is in the park, just below the HWY #9 bridge in Drumheller. Access on the right bank, just behind the Aquatic Center and Tourist Information Centre.

Gradients, Flow Rate and River Volume

This river has an average gradient of approximately 0.8m per kilometer, and does not vary much. The afternoon upstream breeze will have a greater effect on paddling time on any of these reaches than gradient. Flows vary greatly on the Red Deer. At Red Deer over the paddling season, flows may range from less than 20 cms to more than 800 cms, with the normal range being between 30 cms and nearly 130 cms. The velocity of the river at the hydrology station in Red Deer varies from less than 2 kph at 50 cms, to 4 kph at 200 cms, and nearly 8 kph at 800 cms.

Maps

- an up-to-date provincial highways map
- NTS 1:250,000; 82 P - Drumheller and 83 A - Red Deer
- NTS 1:50,000

83 A/5 Red Deer	83 A/3 Delburne
83 A/4 Innisfail (for just 2 km)	83 A/6 Alix
83 A/2 Big Valley	82 P/15 Rumsey
82 P/14 Trochu	82 P/10 Munson
82 P/7 Drumheller	

Camping

There are numerous public campsites along this run, and "unorganized" camping can be had below the high water mark on the banks, on mid-stream islands, and on the crown land that still occupies some quarters above the banks.

The following public campgrounds are available:

- in Red Deer, the Lions Campground just downstream of the 49 Ave. bridge.
- left bank and off the river near the Joffre Bridge
- left bank, upstream of the Content Bridge.
- at Trenville Park.
- left bank, downstream of the McKenzie Crossing Bridge.
- both banks, downstream of the Tolman Bridge.
- left bank, 1 km upstream of the Morin Bridge.
- the right bank below the Bleriot Ferry.
- and just a couple of blocks north of the Hwy. #9 Bridge, off the Dinosaur Trail, in Drumheller

River Notes

This is my "home" river. I grew along and on the "Red." My first overnight canoe trip was with my buddy Greg, from the Content Bridge to the Tolman Bridge, at age 15. In later years I learned my whitewater skills on the upper Red Deer. The Red Deer River has a reach for every paddler. The reaches within this report are for the novice paddler, for the family or youth group looking for a safe and interesting run, and for the naturalist interested in wildlife, fossils, plants, birding -- the works.

When I first began paddling with the Red Deer Canoe & Kayak Club we considered the Red Deer to Joffre run to be the perfect day trip. With good water it takes about 6 hours and it takes you through the "Canyon," home of the Canyon Ski resort. At some water levels there is even a rapid at the top of the canyon, not too far below Burbank: the only spot I have ever lost beer to the river gods! It is usually just a splash in the face, but at high water you should be able to skirt it on the left. Any other rapid or riffle on these reaches can usually be avoided by paddling to the inside of the corner. The river has surprises though: not too many years ago I was on the Content-Trenville run with a group of scouts and we passed a canoe "wrapped" around a mid-stream rock -- the only mid-stream rock that could "grab & wrap" a canoe on the whole 37 km run!

In recent years I have tended to take my Edmonton friends to the upper runs of the Badlands. The Badlands commence about halfway between the Content and Tolman bridges. I always find paddling the Badlands to be pleasant, and the open country provides many opportunities for valley walks with wide vistas. I also tend to go to the Red Deer between early June and early July, for the higher water levels. Over the years I have found that these runs can be slow with low water, but then, some years you just may have to cancel a trip because of late spring flooding. And any river, even "the Red," is dangerous at flood stage.

There is much history along these reaches. In Red Deer you can visit Fort Normandeau (just upstream of the start listed here), a NWMP post established during the Reil Rebellion. Near the Content Bridge is the site of Tail Creek, once the largest Metis buffalo hunting camp in western Canada. Dry Island Buffalo Jump, includes a "jump" that was first used over 3000 years ago. And in Drumheller you can visit the Royal Tyrrell Museum, possibly the finest museum anywhere in the world devoted to Dinosaurs.

One caution must be noted. River ferries such as the Bleriot Ferry can be very hazardous to unwary paddlers. **The river flows under the ferry**. **Do not approach ferries on the upstream side**. Foolish paddlers have been know to try and stop against ferries on the upstream side, and then wonder why their canoe gets "sucked" under! The Bleriot Ferry in particular asks paddlers to wait, and pass only when the ferry is stopped. It is best to pass on the side opposite the ferry. There is a warning sign posted upstream of this ferry (see below).

Bleriot Ferry

Abandoned homestead below Morrin bridge.

North Saskatchewan - Nordegg to Rocky Mountain House

adapted from a report by Mel & Carol Kraft

Ferry Remains, above Ram River

Duration of Tour(s)

* 133.1 km
- half-day, full day or overnight trips are all possible — 3 to 5 days for the whole run.

Classification

1. Overall River: Grade 2
2. Rapids: Class I - III
3. Skill of Paddlers: A good river for Intermediate Open Canadian or practised Novice white water paddlers.

Start

For a 2-3 day trip start 1 km below the Bighorn Dam on the left bank. Most paddlers choose to start at the bridge 10 km south of Nordegg where the Forestry Trunk road crosses the North Saskatchewan River.

For a two day trip start at the Saunders campsite/canoe launch. The turn off on Highway #11 is identified by a *Canoe Launch* sign approximately 60 km west of Rocky Mountain House. It is about 7 km down an improved gravel road through the old site of Saunders to the canoe launch and campsite.

Start at the Horburg campsite/canoe launch for a 1 day trip. To reach this launch site, go west of Rocky Mountain House on Highway #11 about 23 km. Then turn left and go 6 km on the gravel road, passing through Horburg to the AFS (Alberta Forest Service) campsite. The turn is marked with a *Canoe Launch* sign on Highway #11.

An excellent trip for a few hours or even all day with three sets of rapids to play in, is to start at the Rocky Canoe Club access and take out at the Brierley Rapid Access at the Historic Park. Go west of Rocky Mountain House on Highway #11a about 5 km, turn left and go 2 km south to the "T" in the road and turn right. The Rocky Canoe Club access is 1.5 km west of the "T", just before the railway overpass. The Brierley access is 2.0 km east of the "T".

Intermediate Access and Distances

Location	km	km	Access &/or Comments
Access 1 km below Bighorn Dam	0.0		left bank
FTR Bridge south of Nordegg	25.3	25.3	either bank
Saunders Access	54.2	28.9	left bank
Horburg Access	96.7	42.5	left bank
Railway Bridge - Rocky Canoe Club access	124.2	27.5	left bank
National Hist. Site -- boat launch	128.2	4.0	left bank
Highway 11A Bridge in Rocky	133.1	4.9	right bank, under the bridge!

Finish

The old Highway #11a Bridge in Rocky Mountain House. Riverside Park is on the right bank under the bridge. This location has parking, outhouses and is a good site to exit from the river, and to load canoes and gear. **Shuttles** for this run are along the Bighorn Dam Access Road, Hwy. #11, the Forestry Trunk Road, Hwy. #11, the Saunders Access Road, Hwy. #11, Horburg Access Road, the backroad into the Historic site, and Hwy. #11a.

Gradient

Gradients for these runs vary from 1.4 m/km to as much as 4.8 m/km. Much of the river drops at approximately 2 m/km.

Flow Rate and River Volume

Based on nearly 30 years of data, the normal range for June to August flows is from approximately 125 cms to over 450 cms, with peak flows of nearly 1500 cms reported. This river consistently reports maximum flows in late June to early July. At the Rocky Moutain House hydrology station velocity varies from approximately 2.5 km/hr at 150 cms, to 6 km/hr at 400 cms and 8 km/hr at 800 cms.

Camping

Organized:
a) Forestry Trunk Road Bridge - Alymer Staging Area
b) Saunders Campsite/Canoe Launch
c) Horburg Campsite/Canoe Launch

During the early 1980's the Saunders and Horburg Access sites were upgraded to all weather roads and campsites were developed by the Alberta forest service at the request of the Rocky Canoe Club. Paddlers should appreciate their considerate and responsible development of these access/campgrounds.

Wilderness:
Many excellent undeveloped sites are all along the river. The many great camp sites are a real attraction to this reach. Please do not litter and respect private land if you camp at or below the Devil's Elbow.

Maps

Recommended:
NTS. scale 1:50,000
        83 C/8 Nordegg, 83 B/5 Saunders, 83 B/6 Crimson Lake, 83 B/7 Rocky Mountain House
Energy and Natural Resources - Forest District Series - scale of 1"= 3 miles
        Clearwater Sheet
Alternatives:
Provincial Access Series
        83 F/C and 83 G/B
Municipal or County Series:
        M.D. of Clearwater #99, Map #4 (Headwaters to Saunders) & Map #2 (below Saunders to Rocky Mountain House and shows private land)

River Notes

This reach of the North Saskatchewan can be one very popular run, especially on summer long weekends. There have at times been over 200 canoes reported along the river on some long weekend counts. Plan this river for a mid-week trip, to avoid the crowds! It is however a wonderful three to five day trip. Take your time. Do a little hiking in the Gap. A little fishing up Shunda Creek. And, enjoy all the wonderful wilderness campsites between Saunders and Horburg; there seems to be one on at least every second bend!

Rapids and other Hazards

These notes below are the more significant hazards along the river, but are not a complete accounting of every rapid or hazard! Stay Alert!!

km 0 - 31	- the river is very much braided, with many stranded spruce trees in the water, plus logjams and sweepers on most corners or at the head of many gravel bars.
km 36.6	- Dutch creek enters on the left. This marks the beginning of the "Gap" rapids. Beware of the single large rock in mid-stream, opposite Dutch Creek.
km 39.4	- a partial ledge extends out from the left; hold to the right, to the inside of the corner.
km 51.3	- note limestone/tulfa springs on right bank.
km 52.2	- Upper Saunders rapid, rocks and biggest waves are against the cliff, hold to the left.
km 52.9	- Shunda creek enters from left; beware of the strong eddies and boils after the next left corner.
km 53.3	- Saunders Ledge - a significant ledge and keeper/reversal that extends out from the left; hold to the right.
km 88	- Ram river enters from the right, at high water the differential at the boundary can be significant. 2 km downstream note the site of an '83 landslide.
km 102.4	- Devil's Elbow, a long series of shale ledges that can go Class III at some water levels. Hold to the right and one can usually miss all the excitement. Lots of open canoeist swam here!
km 108.2	- Old Stoney, the one big rock mid-stream at the bottom should be avoided; stay to the left. Good camping on right bank.
km 110.3	- Gray's Rapid (below the Green House); hold to the right to avoid.
km 118	- Cow Creek comes in from the right.
km 119 to 120	- Upper Fisher's Rapid. This is the most technical rapid of the whole run to paddle, as it requires that one cross through the waves to take the second corner on the inside. To avoid the worst of these rapids, begin on the right for the right bend, cross over after the worst of the ledges are passed, and then stay to the left for the left bend. Watch for the gravel bar as you finish crossing over.
km 124.9	- Greer Rapid, stay to the right to avoid. These rapids begin 500 m below the railway bridge.
km 126.6	- Lower Fisher's Rapid, again a two part rapid; begin on the left, and then cross over to the right to avoid the final set of ledges and waves that are against the low rock face.
km 128.5	- Brierley's Rapid, can be avoided completely by taking the left channel around the island; at low water stay to the left side of the right channel.

Historical Notes

The Brierley Rapid marks the spot where the fur trade rivals, the North West Company and the Hudson Bay Company, stopped to build their forts. This was the upper limit of easy navigation on the North Saskatchewan River. On the north shore of the river is the Rocky Mountain House National Historic Site. Here the remains of four fur trade posts are preserved for perpetuity. The North West Company was the first to build here and, in 1799, they established Rocky Mountain House on a bench overlooking the rapids. The Hudson Bay Company was quick to follow, a couple of weeks later, and they built Acton House on the flats "within shouting distance from the Nor'Westers". The idea was to attract the trade of the Kootenay Indians from across the mountains who were rumored to have an abundance of furs. The North West Company also wanted a post close to the mountains which their explorer, David Thompson, could use as a base to search for a pass to the Columbia River and eventually to the Pacific Ocean. In 1807 he discovered the Howse Pass. This pass was not used for long, because the Piegan Indians did not want to see their enemies, the Kootenays, armed, and they thus blocked Thompson and his men. He was forced northwards and discovered the Athabasca Pass in 1811. Because this pass was far removed from the Piegans it was favoured as the trade route and Rocky Mountain House was bypassed. In 1821 the two companies amalgamated and one of the forts at Rocky was abandoned. It became an important trade centre since the Piegan traded here and they supplied pemmican which was so necessary for the fur brigades. The last fort closed down in 1875, with the arrival of the Mounted Police in western Canada. It was now safe to build further south and thus be closer to the plains Indians. During the summer you can see different activities throughout the historic site, and wander the trails of the park.

The Rocky / Nordegg area also has a rich history in mining and logging for more than fifty years. Tours are now available through the old coal mine community at Nordegg, a short and worthwhile side trip. Past logging is evident through old winter logging roads throughout the area. An old abandoned ferry, on the right bank about three km upstream of the Ram River, is related to the timber trade.

Where are Finger Rapids? Coyote Rapids? Rivers change, rapids change and those who paddle the river change. The rapids near Rocky Moutain House were first named (in modern times) by Henry Orava and Bryn Thomas in about 1958. They named the rapids with plywood signs along the river so the first racers would know their location. They subsequently named the rapids following the criteria of who owned the adjacent land. Therefore, Upper Fisher's Rapid was named after Art Fisher (deceased). His son Jim now owns the land along the north side of these rapids. Bob Greer and now his son Bill Greer owns the land north of Greer's rapid. Bill Fisher (deceased) and now his son Fred owns the land along the north side of the Lower Fishers's rapid. Cliff Brierley owned the land adjacent to the Brierley's rapid.

Wildlife and Plants
The Rocky / Nordegg area is rich in birds, fish, furbearers and large ungulates. Moose, elk, mule deer, whitetail deer, black bear and grizzly bear all inhabit the area. The nature of the terrain and the hours paddlers normally travel do not lend to many actual observations. Rocky Mountain Bighorn sheep may be spotted in the Gap region. Mel and Carol on one recent trip, identified over 30 species of birds, including golden eagles, bald eagles and osprey. The river has an abundant population of mountain whitefish and a few of several species of trout.

The forest vegetation is dominated by lodgepole pine, aspen and spruce, with the pine the most common. A trip in late September can be spectacular with yellows of the aspen and willows, the reds of birch and red ossier dogwood, the oranges of tamarack, and the various greens of white and black spruce, and pine all along the river.

Upstream Reach
There is a very scenic (Grade 2, with some Class II) easy day run above the Abraham reservoir. This run starts at Saskatchewan crossing and finishes just above the reservoir. One rapid is noted in the picture below. Whirlpool point can provide some excitement — the eddy lines are usually very strong!

Upstream of Whirlpool Point

North Saskatchewan River - Rocky Mountain House to Drayton Valley

Duration of Tour(s)
* 132.5 km
- This run makes for a pleasant, mid-summer, long weekend tour. There is a nice day run from Rocky to the mouth of the Baptiste River at km 40, and access can be made off of the Baptiste road at km 25.5.

A Ceyana Canoe Club group just below Rocky

Classification
1. Overall River: Grade 2
2. Rapids: Class I - II
3. Skill of Paddlers: Intermediate paddler with basic river skills for eddies and ferrying, and wise in the ways for avoiding log jams and sweepers.

Start
The start for this run is under the Highway 11A bridge on the west side of the town of Rocky Mountain House.

Intermediate Access and Distances

Location	km	km	Access &/or Comments
Rocky Mtn. House - Highway 11A	0.0		right bank
Highway #11 Bridge, N. of Rocky	4.5	4.5	right bank
1st access from Baptiste Road	25.5	21.0	right bank
confluence with Baptiste, 2nd access from Baptiste Road	40.0	14.5	left bank, access via oil well road that turns east, just south of the road bridge over the Baptiste.
confluence with the Brazeau	80.4		left side / no access
Blue Rapids (easy Class II)	97.6		often missed! / no access
Rose Creek	110.0		right side / no access
Willey West Campground	132.5	92.5	right side, 400 m below bridge

Finish
The finish is the boat launch within the Willey West Campground. This county campground is below the Hwy. #39 bridge on the east or right bank of the river. Access to the campground is approximately 2 km east and up the hill from the bridge along #39. You must drive right through the campground to reach the boat launching area. **Shuttles** are either driven along the Baptiste Road for the day run, or down Hwy. #22. In '96 we had enough Ceyana paddlers/drivers that we booked the local Rocky Limo' to pick us up at the Willey West Campground and return us to the start -- in style!

Gradient
The average gradient between contour intervals is very consistent on this run, with a total variance from only 1.1 m/km to a maximum of 2.7 m/km, and most of calculated gradients are between 1.5 m/km and 2.2 m/km.

River Volume and Flow Rate

Based on nearly 30 years of data, the normal range for June to August flows is from approximately 125 cms to over 450 cms, with peak flows of nearly 1500 cms reported. This river consistently reports maximum flows in the late June to early July period. At this Rocky Mountain House station, velocity varies from approximately 2.5 km/hr at 150 cms, to 6 km/hr at 400 cms and 8 km/hr at 800 cms.

On a Ceyana Canoe Club trip, Labor Day Weekend '96, we found the river to be at a very nice, modestly low level in Rocky at about 63 cms. After we passed the Brazeau, which had been shut down at the dam and was barely contributing a trickle, we found that we really had to hunt for the deepest channel. An unusual occurrence on the North Saskatchewan.

Maps

- NTS 1:50,000:

83 B/7 Rocky Mountain House	83 B/10 Carlos
83 B/11 Baptiste River	83 B/14 Brazeau
83 G/3 Blue Rapids	83 G/2 Drayton Valley

- an up-to-date Provincial Highways map

Camping

Public campgrounds are available at Riverside Campground, just off of the river at the Highway #11 bridge, and at the finish at the Willey West Campground. This run has a good many fine wilderness campsites, though they are not as frequent as upstream of Horburg.

River Notes

This is a very fine run later in the summer for novice paddlers that have mastered the North Saskatchewan closer to Edmonton. Much of the run is braided, so paddlers must always be alert for logjams and sweepers. On our '96 run mentioned above, not far above the Baptiste River we came across a short section where the river had cut a new channel across a meander bend. As is common in this situation, the entry to the new channel was nearly choked with logjams, and the river through the new channel was fast and overhung on the outside of the bends with many sweepers. On an earlier trip that summer, another club member actually retrieved a lost canoe from a logjam on this new channel.

The rapids on this run are usually formed at the gravel lined chutes, or by the fast water on the outside of bends that may be running over bedrock shale ledges. There are some spots with larger boulders that have to be avoided.
Generally an alert paddler, even a novice with basic control skills, has little trouble negotiating these problems.

Paddlers should recognize the sense of history on this run. Voyagers and York Boat men regularly plied this run upstream and down for nearly ninety years in the fur trade era. Not only was there the major fur houses just upstream of Rocky, but Boggy Hall existed for a short period, some 16 km below the Brazeau confluence.

Battle River - some general thoughts

The Battle river winds (it is a "misfit stream") from Battle Lake west of Pigeon Lake in Central Alberta, through Ponoka, then north towards Camrose past the Hobbema Reserves. Near Gwynne it turns east and heads past Forestburg, Hardisty, Wainwright and finally empties into the North Saskatchewan at Battelford, Saskatchewan. Over the years I have paddled this stream near Battle Lake, in Ponoka, and once on a mildly exciting run near Gwynne. Various friends have taken extended overnight trips on different sections. To my mind it is an underutilized local paddling resource. It can also be a slow, winding paddle interrupted by beaver dams, fallen logs that completely block the stream and barbed-wire fences. I have never calculated the gradient, but, at one time I understood that local Camrose paddlers were using the section near Gwynne as a spring whitewater training run. We followed. Much of the river was a fun run and was made memorable by the many spawning suckers, and then the new channel! In mid-trip we rounded a corner and the river disappeared into a gravel pit. It exited the gravel pit through a willow swamp that necessitated waist deep wading and pushing through the tree growth. It rather extended our anticipated paddling time!

For most of its length the Battle flows in an ancient glacial spillway, and is thus characterized as a "misfit" stream. This is what leads to its winding nature. If you are interested in paddling this river I have listed the required maps for Alberta below. I would certainly allow generous time for any run, and would expect that 15 to 25 km per day may be a reasonable goal. It is a small river that will allow you some great opportunities to observe wildlife. If you complete a trip I would really like to hear from you.

Maps
- NTS 1:50,000 N.T.S (from upstream to downstream, west to east): 83 B/16, 83 A/13, 83 A/12, 83 A/11, 83 A/14, 83 A/15, 83 A/10, 83 A/9, 83 A/8, 73 D/5, 73 D/6, 73 D11, 73 D/14, 73 D/15, 73 E/2, 73 E/1, 73 D/16. Be sure to consult the *1:50,000 Index Map #2* to choose only the sheets that you require.
- an up-to-date Provincial Highways map

East and North of Edmonton — rivers and lakes

Athabasca River - Whitecourt to the Vega (Klondike) Ferry

Duration of Tour(s)
* 123 km - This reach can make a very nice 3 to 4 day canoe trip, but could be "rushed" in less!

Classification
1. Overall River: easy Grade 2
2. Rapids: Class I
3. Skill of Paddlers: Practised Novice with basic river skills

Start
The start is at the Whitecourt boat launch at the mouth of the McLeod River. Exit east off of Highway #43, just south of the Athabasca River Bridge. Follow the gravel road east along the Athabasca and down to the boat launch.

Intermediate Access and Distances

Location	km	km	Access &/or Comments
Whitecourt - mouth of McLeod R.	0.0		right bank of Athabasca
N. of Blue Ridge - #658 Bridge	21.0	21.0	
Fort Assiniboine - #33 Bridge	82.0	61.0	
Vega / Klondike Ferry	123.0	41.0	either bank

Finish
The finish for this run is at the Vega Ferry on Secondary Highway #661.

Gradient
The overall average gradient for this run is .8 m/km.

River Volume and Flow Rate
From 1960 to 1988 the Hydrology Station near Whitecourt has reported a normal summer flow for mid-May to late August of between 250 cms to 800 cms, and peak flows of over 2200 cms! At this station velocity varies from approximately 1.5 km/hr at 200 cms, 5 km/hr at 1000 cms, to 9 km/hr at 3000 cms.

Maps
- an up-to-date Provincial Highways Map
- NTS 1:250,000 sheet: 83 J Whitecourt

Camping
There are public campgrounds in Whitecourt, Fort Assiniboine and at the Vega Ferry. Like all our big rivers in this province, as they slow down, campsites tend to become less plentiful. Small groups at lower water levels may be able to camp almost anywhere. At higher water levels, and with larger groups, start your campsite search early each afternoon, and when you find a marginal one, do not expect a "better one" on the next bend!

River Notes

Below Whitecourt this river slows down. For much of the distance it meanders and has many mid-stream islands. These, of course, tend to harbor logjams on their upstream "prow." Sweepers can still be a hazard. The fishing can be good on this run! This is a good, mid to late season run for the developing paddler.

Pembina and Athabasca Rivers - Flatbush to Chisholm Mills

Duration of Tour(s)
*48.4 km
 - a very pleasant overnight tour for novice paddlers at medium to medium-low water levels. There is a one day paddle down to the confluence (km 26.6).

Classification
1. Overall River: Grade 1
2. Rapids: Class I to very easy II at some water levels
3. Skill of Paddlers: Novice paddlers with basic moving water skills.

Start
The start for this paddle is at the bridge approximately 1.4 km south and 3.7 km west of Flatbush. Flatbush itself is 3.2 km west of Highway #44 and 67 km north of Westlock.

Intermediate Access and Distances
There is one access possible at the confluence with the Athabasca (km 26.6). A rough road leads for 500 m up to a good wellsite road that is a continuation of the road from the start. Head west across the bridge, turn right and follow the road almost to the end. This access is between the Athabasca and the Pembina.

Finish
The finish for this reach is just beyond the town Chisholm Mills. Drive through the town, across the railway line and pass the sawmill down to the river. Access is on river right.

Gradients
This is a gentle downhill run, the first 12 km on the Pembina drops at .6 m/km, then down to the confluence the gradient approaches 1 m/km. On the Athabasca the gradient is approximately .4 m/km.

River Volume and Flow Rate
The nearest hydrology station with published data, on the Pembina, for this run is at Jarvie, some 30 km or so upstream "as the crow flies."   With nearly 30 years of data, this station has reported that the normal flows for late April to early September range from 15 cms to nearly 160 cms, average flows in this period range from 20 cms to 70 cms. Spring Snow Melt is significant to this river as the river has two pronounced high flow periods, late April and mid-June to late August. Peak flows in each of these periods have approached 1000 cms. At normal flows the velocity of this river ranges from less the 2 km/hr to over 3 km/hr.

Maps
- NTS 1:50,000: 83 J/9 Flatbush and 83 J/16 Chisholm
- Alberta Environment Resource Access Map 1:50,000: 83-J/9 and 83-J/16
- an up-to-date Provincial Highways Map

Camping
There are no Public Campground along this run or in the immediate vicinity. The run is pretty much away from any farmlands, and wilderness campsites do occur. Unfortunately like most of our Aspen-Parkland, low gradient streams, campsites can be harder to find than along our foothills streams.

River Notes

This is a gentle stream that can be paddled surprisingly late into the season. My only experiences on this Flatbush reach have been on fall hunting adventures. My memories are of cool, gray early mornings, with the morning fog slowly burning off for bright sunny fall days. Days colored by the sun, the golden aspens, the reds of birch and dogwood, the orange of tamaracks and the various greens of spruce and pine. On my second run, at about the 5 km point the fog seemed very thick, then we noticed the odor. Fire! We searched just a little and found a ground fire that had consumed an area equal to about two houses. With plastic paddle and 76 bailer loads of water we did our best to chop away and wet down the perimeter. Later in the evening, on our return to Edmonton, I reported the fire, and a couple of weeks later received a nice thank-you note from the District Forest Superintendent, and a copy of the history of the Alberta Forest Service! Good deeds do pay!

During my employment at the University of Alberta I had the pleasure of mixing a paddling course with an Alberta History course. On our paddle from Fort Assinboine we stopped at the mouth of the Pembina, and Professor Babcock, was able to take the crew into the site of an early and short-lived fur trade post. Unfortunately the only visible remnant was the collapsed hole of the cellar.

Sand River - from Highway #55 to the confluence with the Beaver River

Bob and Eric on the Sand River

Duration of Tour(s)
* 21.5 km
- a very nice day tour.

Classification
1. Overall River:	Grade 2
2. Rapids:	Class I to II
3. Skill of Paddlers:	Intermediate at medium to high water, novice with basic river skills at medium to low water levels.

Start
The start for this run is at the Highway #55 Bridge just north and east of Truman, or west of Iron River.

Finish
The finish for this run is 3.2 km south of Iron River, then 4.8 km west, and then another 5 km south and west on an unimproved (beware in wet weather) road down to the confluence of the Sand and Beaver Rivers.

Gradient
This run, on the 1:50,000 sheet, the river crosses three contour intervals of 25 ft, for average gradients of .83 and .85 m/km.

River Volume and Flow Rate
The *Streamflow Facts* sheet for the Sand River, is taken for the hydrology station near the confluence, and reports data for the years 1967 to 1988. Normal flows from mid-April to mid-August range from about 8 cms to 55 cms. Like the lower Pembina the largest flows have been reported in late April to early May, with a second peak in early to mid-July. Maximum reported flows have reached nearly 200 cms.

Maps
- NTS 1:50,000: 73 L/6 Goodridge (for the River) and 73 L/7 Bonnyville (for the shuttle)
- an up-to-date Provincial Highways Map

Camping
There are a number of Public Campgrounds in the area, five on Moose Lake, and one north of Iron River. My favorite is Moose Lake Provincial Park. I just love the Jack Pine, reindeer moss and sand dunes that dominate this park. For wilderness camping the west bank of the Sand River is still relatively wilderness; the long series of stabilized sand dunes makes for poor farmland, and some nice campsites.

River Notes
I have to confess to just one run on this river in mid-July. It was one of the first runs we "farmed" young Eric "out" to paddle with another club member, the late Bob Turner. We all had a wonderful time drifting the easy reaches, and dodging the boulders in the occasional bits of swifter water. At higher water there could be some tricky boulder dodging, and even a sweeper or logjam to avoid.

As I peruse old reports and the *Bedrock Topography* map that I have collected I see that previous authors and map makers have reported as many as 13 rapids on this reach. None of these are really significant, just the boulder gardens and minor chutes as reported above. This is a relatively low gradient stream! But then, it only takes one boulder to "wrap" a canoe. Yes, there are times that one must be awake on the Sand River. One spot to note is the old bridge piers that occur at about km 1.5. These can be tricky at some water levels.

Our memories are not only of a pleasant paddle, but of a warm summer day with the bees buzzing through the multitudes of flowers, and us chasing a series of Great Blue Herons down the river, with the occasional osprey stealing a fish from just in front of us. This is a fine run and well worth the driving time, especially if combined with a day of drifting through the wet lands around Moose Lake.

Other Reaches

Past guides have encouraged paddlers to start as high as Wolf Lake on the Sand river system and unfortunately there have not been many positive reports of the paddle/drag/wade out of Wolf Lake. Various reaches on the Beaver are also possible, though it is much like the Battle River, a "misfit" stream flowing, or rather meandering, through an old glacial spillway. It can be a nice paddle at the right water levels, and if your goal is not great distance!

Moose Lake - near Bonnyville

Introduction
Moose Lake is one of the many fine lakes in the "Lakeland" region of north eastern Alberta. Moose lake has five campgrounds on it shores, and offers many fine sandy beaches, good fishing, and wet lands for exploring and birding.

Duration of Tour(s)
* up to 17 km or more!
A variety of part-day tours are available from or between the various access points on the lake.

Classification
Lake, with the risk of strong winds.

Start & Finish
Moose Lake is approximately 240 km north-east of Edmonton, and just minutes west of Bonnyville. Campgrounds or picnic areas with boat launches, beaches or piers are available at:

     1 - Moose Lake Provincial Park on the north shore off of Secondary Hwy . #660,
     2 - Franchere Bay Provincial Recreation Area on the north-west shore off of Hwy. #660,
     3 - Pelican Point Park on the west shore/south-east Shore of Franchere Bay,
     4 - Bonnyville Beach on the south-east shore, off of Hwy. #28,
     5 - Vezeau Beach Recreation Area on the north-east shore/ south shore of Vezeau Bay, off of Hwy. #28.

Distance Summary
1 - From Bonnyville Beach to Franchere Bay Provincial Recreation Area, along the south shore:
     - 6 km   - road access from the south
     - 12 km - Pelican Point Park
     - 17 km - Franchere Bay Provincial Recreation Area
2 - From the east pier in Moose Lake Provincial Park to Vezeau Beach Rec. Area., along north and east shores - 9.5 km.
3 - From the west pier in Moose Lake Provincial Park to Franchere Bay Provincial Rec. Area, along the north shore - 6 km.

Maps
- N.T.S. 1:50,000: 73 L/2 Muriel Lake, 73 L/6 Goodridge and 73 L/7 Bonnyville
- a good up-to-date Provincial Highways Map

Camping
1 - Moose Lake Provincial Park (my first choice!)   2 - Franchere Bay Provincial Recreation Area
3 - Pelican Point Park   4 -Vezeau Beach Provincial Recreation Area

Tour Notes:
Moose Lake is a fine weekend destination spot. The sandy beaches, the "jack" and pickerel fishing and the various wetlands and shallows on the lake's perimeter all make for good "paddling excuses." Pelicans and many other birds frequent the lake. And one should "stick" their canoe into the Moose Lake and Thin Lake rivers (Franchere Bay) just to say that they too have paddled a portion of the old historic fur trade route that once connected the Athabasca River with the North Saskatchewan River, through Lac la Biche. One caution: near the parks you will be sharing this lake with many others, some of questionable boat operating skills!

Appendix A - Safety Considerations

Safety Code of the American Whitewater Affiliation
Four Decades of Service to the Paddlers of America
"Our mission is to conserve and restore America's whitewater resources and to enhance opportunities to enjoy them safely."

Adopted 1959
Revised 1989
Charlie Walbridge: Revision Chairman
Pete Skinner: Production Coordinator
Mac Thornton: Legal Advisor

This code has been prepared using the best available information and has been reviewed by a broad cross section of whitewater experts. The code, however, is only a collection of guidelines; attempts to minimize risks should be flexible, not constrained by a rigid set of rules. Varying conditions and group goals may combine with unpredictable circumstances to require alternate procedures. For additional copies please write: American Whitewater Affiliation, PO Box 85, Phoenicia, NY 12464 (email: 74663.2104@compuserve.com)

I. PERSONAL PREPAREDNESS AND RESPONSIBILITY

1. *Be a competent swimmer*, with the ability to handle yourself underwater.

2. *Wear a life jacket (or Personal Flotation Device {PFD} designed for paddlers)*. A snugly-fitting vest-type life preserver offers back and shoulder protection as well as the flotation needed to swim safely in whitewater.

3. *Wear a solid, correctly-fitted helmet when upsets are likely*. This is essential in kayaks or covered canoes, and recommended for open canoeists using thigh straps and rafters running steep drops.

4. *Do not boat out of control.* Your skills should be sufficient to stop or reach shore before reaching danger. Do not enter a rapid unless you are reasonably sure that you can run it safely or swim it without injury.

5. Whitewater rivers contain *many hazards* which are not always easily recognized. The following are the most frequent killers.
   5.A. **HIGH WATER**. The river's speed and power increase tremendously as the flow increases, raising the difficulty of most rapids. Rescue becomes progressively harder as the water rises, adding to the danger. Floating debris and strainers make even an easy rapid quite hazardous. It is often misleading to judge the river level at the put in, since a small rise in a wide, shallow place will be multiplied many times where the river narrows. Use reliable gauge information whenever possible, and be aware that sun on snowpack, hard rain, and upstream dam releases may greatly increase the flow.
   5.B. **COLD**. Cold drains your strength and robs you of the ability to make sound decisions on matters affecting your survival. Cold water immersion, because of the initial shock and the rapid heat loss which follows, is especially dangerous. Dress appropriately for bad weather or sudden immersion in the water. When the water temperature is less than 50 degree F., a wetsuit or drysuit is essential for protection if you swim. Next best is wool or pile clothing under a waterproof shell. In this case, you should also carry waterproof matches and a change of clothing in a waterproof bag. If, after prolonged exposure, a person experiences uncontrollable shaking, loss of coordination, or difficulty speaking, he or she is hypothermic, and needs your assistance.

5.C. **STRAINERS.** Brush, fallen trees, bridge pilings, undercut rocks or anything else which allows river current to sweep through can pin boats and boaters against the obstacle. Water pressure on anything trapped this way can be overwhelming. Rescue is often extremely difficult. Pinning may occur in fast current, with little or no whitewater to warn of the danger.

5.D. **HOLES, AND HYDRAULICS.** When water drops over a obstacle, it curls back on itself, forming a strong upstream current which may be capable of holding a boat or swimmer. Some holes make for excellent sport. Others are proven killers. *Paddlers who cannot recognize the difference should avoid all but the smallest holes.* Hydraulics around man-made dams must be treated with utmost respect regardless of their height or the level of the river. Despite their seemingly benign appearance, they can create an almost escape-proof trap. The swimmers *only exit* from the "drowning machine" is to dive below the surface where the downstream current is flowing beneath the reversal.

5.E. **BROACHING.** When a boat is pushed sideways against a rock by strong current, it may collapse and wrap. This is especially dangerous to kayak and decked canoe paddlers; these boats will collapse and the combination of indestructible hulls and tight outfitting may create a deadly trap. Even without entrapment, releasing pinned boats can be extremely time-consuming and dangerous. To avoid pinning, throw your weight downstream towards the rock, and lean your boat onto the rock. This allows the current to slide harmlessly underneath the hull.

6. *Boating alone is discouraged.* The minimum party is three people and/or two craft.

7. Have a frank *knowledge of your boating ability*, and don't attempt rivers or rapids which lie beyond that ability.

7.A. Develop the *paddling skills and teamwork* required to match the river you plan to boat. Most good paddlers develop skills gradually, and attempts to advance quickly will compromise your safety and enjoyment.

7.B. Be in *good physical and mental condition*, consistent with the difficulties which may be expected. Make adjustments for loss of skills due to age, health, fitness. Any health limitations must be explained to your fellow paddlers prior to starting the trip.

8. Be practised in *self-rescue*, including escape from an overturned craft. The Eskimo Roll is strongly recommended for decked boaters who run rapids Class IV or greater, or who paddle in cold environmental conditions.

9. Be trained in *rescue skills, CPR, and first aid* with special emphasis on the recognizing and treating of hypothermia. It may save your friend's life.

10. Carry *equipment* needed for unexpected emergencies, including foot wear which will protect your feet when walking out, a throw rope, knife, whistle, and waterproof matches. If you wear eyeglasses, tie them on and carry a spare pair on long trips. Bring cloth repair tape on short runs, and a full repair kit on isolated rivers. Do not wear bulky jackets, ponchos, heavy boots, or anything else which could reduce your ability to survive a swim.

11. Despite the mutually supportive group structure described in this code, *individual paddlers are ultimately responsible for their own safety, and must assume sole responsibility for the following decisions*:

11.A. The decision to participate on any trip. This includes an evaluation of the expected difficulty of the rapids under the conditions existing at the time of the put-in.

11.B. The selection of appropriate equipment, including a boat design suited to their skills and the appropriate rescue and survival gear.

11.C. The decision to scout any rapid, and to run or portage according to their best judgment. Other members of the group may offer advice, but paddlers should resist pressure from anyone to paddle beyond their skills. It is also their responsibility to decide whether to pass up any walk-out or take-out opportunity.

11.D. All trip participants should consistently evaluate their own and their group's safety, voicing their concerns when appropriate and following what they believe to be the best course of action. Paddlers are encouraged to speak with anyone whose actions on the water are dangerous, whether they are a part of your group or not.

II. BOAT AND EQUIPMENT PREPAREDNESS

1. *Test new and different equipment* under familiar conditions before relying on it for difficult runs. This is especially true when adopting a new boat design or outfitting system. Low volume craft may present additional hazards to inexperienced or poorly conditioned paddlers.

2. Be sure your boat and gear are in *good repair* before starting a trip. The more isolated and difficult the run, the more rigorous this inspection should be.

3. Install *flotation bags* in non-inflatable craft, securely fixed in each end, designed to displace as much water as possible. Inflatable boats should have multiple air chambers and be test inflated before launching.

4. Have strong, properly sized *paddles or oars* for controlling your craft. Carry sufficient spares for the length and difficulty of the trip.

5. Outfit your boat safely. The *ability to exit your boat quickly* is an essential component of safety in rapids. It is your responsibility to see that there is absolutely nothing to cause entrapment when coming free of an upset craft. This includes:
   5.A. Spray covers which won't release reliably or which release prematurely.
   5.B. Boat outfitting too tight to allow a fast exit, especially in low volume kayaks or decked canoes. This includes low hung thwarts in canoes lacking adequate clearance for your feet and kayak footbraces which fail or allow your feet to become wedged under them.
   5.C. Inadequately supported decks which collapse on a paddler's legs when a decked boat is pinned by water pressure. Inadequate clearance with the deck because of your size or build.
   5.D. Loose ropes which cause entanglement. Beware of any length of loose line attached to a whitewater boat. All items must be tied tightly and excess line eliminated; painters, throw lines, and safety rope systems must be completely and effectively stored. Do not knot the end of a rope, as it can get caught in cracks between rocks.

6. Provide *ropes* which permit you to hold on to your craft so that it may be rescued. The following methods are recommended:
   6.A. Kayaks and covered canoes should have grab loops of 1/4" + rope or equivalent webbing sized to admit a normal sized hand. Stern painters are permissible if properly secured.
   6.B. Open canoes should have securely anchored bow and stern painters consisting of 8 - 10 feet of 1/4" + line. These must be secured in such a way that they are readily accessible, but cannot come loose accidentally. Grab loops are acceptable, but are more difficult to reach after an upset.
   6.C. Rafts and dories may have taut perimeter lines threaded through the loops provided. Footholds should be designed so that a paddler's feet cannot be forced through them, causing entrapment. Flip lines should be carefully and reliably stowed.

7. Know your craft's carrying capacity, and how added loads affect boat handling in whitewater. Most rafts have a minimum crew size which can be added to on day trips or in easy rapids. Carrying more than two paddlers in an open canoe when running rapids is not recommended.

8. Car top racks must be strong and attach positively to the vehicle. Lash your boat to each crossbar, then tie the ends of the boats directly to the bumpers for added security. This arrangement should survive all but the most violent vehicle accident.

III. GROUP PREPAREDNESS AND RESPONSIBILITY

1. *Organization.* A river trip should be regarded as a common adventure by all participants, except on instructional or commercially guided trips as defined below. Participants share the responsibility for the conduct of the trip, and each participant is individually responsible for judging his or her own capabilities and for his or her own safety as the trip progresses. Participants are encouraged (but are not obligated) to offer advice and guidance for the independent consideration and judgment of others.

2. *River Conditions.* The group should have a reasonable knowledge of the difficulty of the run. Participants should evaluate this information and adjust their plans accordingly. If the run is exploratory or no one is familiar with the river, maps and guidebooks, if available, should be examined. The group should secure accurate flow information; the more difficult the run, the more important this will be. Be aware of possible changes in river level and how this will affect the difficulty of the run. If the trip involves tidal stretches, secure appropriate information on tides.

3. *Group equipment* should be suited to the difficulty of the river. The group should always have a throw line available, and one line per boat is recommended on difficult runs. The list may include: carbiners, prussick loops, first aid kit, flashlight, folding saw, fire starter, guidebooks, maps, food, extra clothing, and any other rescue or survival items suggested by conditions. Each item is not required on every run, and this list is not meant to be a substitute for good judgment.

4. *Keep the group compact*, but maintain sufficient spacing to avoid collisions. If the group is large, consider dividing into smaller groups or using the *"Buddy System"* as an additional safeguard. Space yourselves closely enough to permit good communication, but not so close as to interfere with one another in rapids.

   4.A. The lead paddler sets the pace. When in front, do not get in over your head. Never run drops when you cannot see a clear route to the bottom or, for advanced paddlers, a sure route to the next eddy. *When in doubt, stop and scout.*

   4.B. *Keep track of all group members.* Each boat keeps the one behind it in sight, stopping if necessary. Know how many people are in your group and take head counts regularly. No one should paddle ahead or walk out without first informing the group. Weak paddlers should stay at the center of a group, and not allow themselves to lag behind. If the group is large and contains a wide range of abilities, a designated ``Sweep Boat" should bring up the rear.

   4.C. *Courtesy.* On heavily used rivers, do not cut in front of a boater running a drop. Always look upstream before leaving eddies to run or play. Never enter a crowded drop or eddy when no room for you exists. Passing other groups in a rapid may be hazardous: it is often safer to wait upstream until the group ahead has passed.

5. *Float plan.* If the trip is into a wilderness area or for an extended period, plans should be filed with a responsible person who will contact the authorities if you are overdue. It may be wise to establish checkpoints along the way where civilization could be contacted if necessary. Knowing the location of possible help and preplanning escape routes can speed rescue.

6. *Drugs.* The use of alcohol or mind altering drugs before or during river trips is not recommended. It dulls reflexes, reduces decision making ability, and may interfere with important survival reflexes.

7. *Instructional or Commercially Guided Trips.* In contrast to the common adventure trip format, in these trip formats, a boating instructor or commercial guide assumes some of the responsibilities normally exercised by the group as a whole, as appropriate under the circumstances. These formats recognize that instructional or commercially guided trips may involve participants who lack significant experience in whitewater. However, as a participant acquires experience in whitewater, he or she takes on increasing responsibility for his or her own safety, in accordance with what he or she knows or should know as a result of that increased experience. Also, as in all trip formats, every participant must realize and assume the risks associated with the serious hazards of whitewater rivers. It is advisable for instructors and commercial guides to acquire trip or personal liability insurance:

    7.A. An "`instructional trip'" is characterized by a clear teacher/pupil relationship, where the primary purpose of the trip is to teach boating skills, and which is conducted for a fee.

    7.B. A "commercially guided trip'" is characterized by a licensed, professional guide conducting trips for a fee.

IV. GUIDELINES FOR RIVER RESCUE

1. Recover from an upset with an Eskimo roll whenever possible. Evacuate your boat immediately if there is imminent danger of being trapped against rocks, brush, or any other kind of strainer.

2. If you swim, hold on to your boat. It has much flotation and is easy for rescuers to spot. Get to the upstream end so that you cannot be crushed between a rock and your boat by the force of the current. Persons with good balance may be able to climb on top of a swamped kayak or flipped raft and paddle to shore.

3. Release your craft if this will improve your chances, especially if the water is cold or dangerous rapids lie ahead. Actively attempt self-rescue whenever possible by swimming for safety. Be prepared to assist others who may come to your aid.

    3.A. When swimming in shallow or obstructed rapids, lie on your back with feet held high and pointed downstream. Do not attempt to stand in fast moving water; if your foot wedges on the bottom, fast water will push you under and keep you there. Get to slow or very shallow water before attempting to stand or walk. Look ahead! Avoid possible pinning situations including undercut rocks, strainers, downed trees, holes, and other dangers by swimming away from them.

    3.B. If the rapids are deep and powerful, roll over onto your stomach and swim aggressively for shore. Watch for eddies and slackwater and use them to get out of the current. Strong swimmers can effect a powerful upstream ferry and get to shore fast. If the shores are obstructed with strainers or under cut rocks, however, it is safer to "`ride the rapid out" until a safer escape can be found.

4. If others spill and swim, *go after the boaters first*. Rescue boats and equipment only if this can be done safely. While participants are encouraged (but not obligated) to assist one another to the best of their ability, they should do so only if they can, in their judgment, do so safely. The first duty of a rescuer is not to compound the problem by becoming another victim.

5. The use of rescue lines requires training; uninformed use may cause injury. Never tie yourself into either end of a line without a reliable quick-release system. Have a knife handy to deal with unexpected entanglement. Learn to place set lines effectively, to throw accurately, to belay effectively, and to properly handle a rope thrown to you.

6. When reviving a drowning victim, be aware that *cold water* may greatly extend survival time underwater. Victims of hypothermia may have depressed vital signs so they look and feel dead. Don't give up; continue CPR for as long as possible without compromising safety.

V. UNIVERSAL RIVER SIGNALS

STOP: Potential hazard ahead. Wait for **"all clear"** signal before proceeding, or scout ahead. Form a horizontal bar with your outstretched arms, and paddle if available. Those seeing the signal should pass it back to others in the party.

HELP/EMERGENCY: Assist the signaler as quickly as possible. Give three long blasts on a police whistle while waving a paddle, helmet or life vest over your head, in a vertical circular action. If a whistle is not available, use the visual signal alone. A whistle is best carried on a lanyard attached to your life vest.

ALL CLEAR: Come ahead (in the absence of other directions proceed down the center). Form a vertical bar with your paddle or one arm held high above your head. Paddle blade should be turned flat for maximum visibility. To signal direction or a preferred course through a rapid, or around an obstruction, lower the previously vertical **"all clear"** by 45 degrees toward the side of the river with the preferred route. **Never point** toward the obstacle you wish to avoid.

GROUP UP: use repeat short blasts, or "chirps" on the whistle to indicate that the lead canoe should stop and wait for the sweep canoe. This signal is repeated by all boats until all paddlers have received it.

IV. INTERNATIONAL SCALE OF RIVER DIFFICULTY

This is the American version of a rating system used to compare river difficulty throughout the world. This system is not exact; rivers do not always fit easily into one category, and regional or individual interpretations may cause misunderstandings. It is no substitute for a guidebook or accurate first-hand descriptions of a run.

Paddlers attempting difficult runs in an unfamiliar area should act cautiously until they get a feel for the way the scale is interpreted locally. River difficulty may change each year due to fluctuations in water level, downed trees, geological disturbances, or bad weather. **Stay alert for unexpected problems!**

As river difficulty increases, the danger to swimming paddlers becomes more severe. As rapids become longer and more continuous, the challenge increases. There is a difference between running an occasional Class IV rapid and dealing with an entire river of this category. Allow an extra margin of safety between skills and river ratings when the water is cold or if the river itself is remote and inaccessible.

THE SIX DIFFICULTY CLASSES FOR RAPIDS:

Class I: Easy. Some what fast moving water with riffles and small waves. Few obstructions, all obvious and easily missed with little training. Risk to swimmers is slight; self-rescue is easy.

Class II: Novice. Straightforward rapids with wide, clear channels which are evident without scouting. Occasional maneuvering may be required, but rocks and medium sized waves are easily missed by trained paddlers. Swimmers are seldom injured and group assistance, while helpful, is seldom needed.

Class III: Intermediate. Rapids with moderate, irregular waves which may be difficult to avoid and which can swamp an open canoe. Complex maneuvers in fast current and good boat control in tight passages or around ledges are often required; large waves or strainers may be present but are easily avoided. Strong eddies and powerful current effects can be found, particularly on large-volume rivers. Scouting is advisable for inexperienced parties. Injuries while swimming are rare; self-rescue is usually easy but group assistance may be required to avoid long swims.

Class IV: Advanced. Intense, powerful but predictable rapids requiring precise boat handling in turbulent water. Depending on the character of the river, it may feature large, unavoidable waves and holes or constricted passages demanding fast maneuvers under pressure. A fast, reliable eddy turn is needed to initiate maneuvers, scout rapids, or rest. Rapids may require "must" moves above dangerous hazards. Scouting is necessary the first time down. Risk of injury to swimmers is moderate to high, and water conditions may make self-rescue difficult. Group assistance for rescue is often essential but requires practised skills. A strong Eskimo roll is highly recommended.

Class V: Expert. Extremely long, obstructed, or very violent rapids which expose a paddler to above average endangerment. Drops may contain large, unavoidable waves and holes or steep, congested chutes with complex, demanding routes. Rapids may continue for long distances between pools, demanding a high level of fitness. What eddies exist may be small, turbulent, or difficult to reach. At the high end of the scale, several of these factors may be combined. Scouting is mandatory but often difficult. Swims are dangerous, and rescue is difficult even for experts. A very reliable Eskimo roll, proper equipment, extensive experience, and practiced rescue skills are essential for survival.

Class VI: Extreme. One grade more difficult than Class V. These runs often exemplify the extremes of difficulty, unpredictability and danger. The consequences of errors are very severe and rescue may be impossible. For teams of experts only, at favorable water levels, after close personal inspection and taking all precautions. This class does not represent drops thought to be unrunnable, but may include rapids which are only occasionally run.

Appendix B - Local Clubs, Educational Programs & Rentals

All the canoe clubs in Alberta are largely, or completely volunteer "run." Membership and executive members change, and the following will soon be out of date. If these contacts do not work, try reaching the club through the local municipal recreation department, local outdoor sporting goods store, or swimming pool (we all book pool time in the winter!).

Bow Waters Canoe Club
P.O. Box 697, Postal Station J
Calgary, Alberta, T2A 4X8
Clubhouse phone @ 235-2922

Calgary Area Outdoor Council
1111 Memorial Dr., N.W.
Calgary, Alberta, T2N 3E4
phone @ 403-270-2262
e-mail: caoc@freenet.calgary.ab.ca

Calgary Canoe Club
Box 36004 or 6449 Crowshild Tr., S.W.
Calgary, Alberta, T3E 7C6
phone @ 403-246-5757

Ceyana Canoe Club
Box 72023 Ottewell Postal Outlet
Edmonton, Alberta, T6B 0J1
Membership Chair (1998) Dave @ 437-6328

Edmonton White Water Paddlers
c/o 11215 - 53 Ave.
Edmonton, Alberta, T6H 0S6
Dale @ 434-9192

Friends of the River
9726 - 158 Street
Edmonton, Alberta, T5P 2X1
Bob @ 489-8846

Hinton Strokers
P.O. Box 5124
Hinton, Alberta, T7V 1X3
Greg @ 865-5743
clubhouse @ 865-5335

Jasper River Runners
Box 2443
Jasper, Alberta, T0E 1E0

North West Voyageurs
Box 1341
Edmonton, Alberta, T5J 2N2
Membership Chair (1997)
Madeline @ 489-8723

Red Deer Canoe and Kayak Club

Rocky Canoe Club
P.O. Box 995
Rocky Mtn. House, Alberta, T0M 1T0
Mel & Carol @ 845-4814

Edmonton Parks and Recreation (Community Services)
River Valley Center @ 496-7275

Strathcona Wilderness Centre
in the County of Strathcona, 16 km east of Sherwood Park on Baseline Road (922-3939)

YoWoChAs
YWCA Outdoor Education Center
east of Fallis, on the North Shore of Lake Wabamun (892-2660)

Shipwreck Boat Rentals
12704 - Yellowhead Trail (454-7887) or
9065-63 Ave. (469-8266)

Shipshape Boat & Canoe Rentals
4433 - 118 Ave. (474-6970)

University of Alberta -- Campus Outdoor Centre
Northwest Corner of the Butterdome (492-2767)

If you have a paddling club or program that you would like to be included in future editions, or corrections, please contact the author.

Appendix C - Selected Canoeing Manuals and "Web" Resources

Books and Manuals:

American Red Cross (1977) *Canoeing*, **Doubleday & Co., Garden City, New York**
This is the classic text for canoeing and covers many aspects that other manuals completely forget, such as canoe sailing and poling. Some of the material is becoming a little dated, but still a text I often refer to. If you can find it — buy it!

Gullion, L. (1987) *Canoeing and Kayaking - Instruction Manual*, **American Canoe Association, Newington, Virginia**
This book is a little thin as an instructors manual but has some very good discussions on basic stroke techniques, and introductory river techniques.

Mason, B. (1980) *Path of the Paddle - an illustrated guide to the art of canoeing*, **Van Nostrand Reinhold Ltd., Toronto, Ontario**
This is the Canadian Classic already. Bill passed away some years ago, and his son Paul, and even better paddler, has recently brought out a revised edition. A must have, for every paddler!

Mason, B. (1988) *Song of the Paddle - an illustrated guide to wilderness camping*, **Key Porter Books, Toronto, Ontario**
This is Bill's other classic, a guide to canoe camping. The information is good, and the pictures and illustrations are wonderful.

Ray, S. (1992) *The Canoe Handbook*, **Stackpole Books, Harrisburg, Pa.**
Slim Ray is a long time American Paddler and Instructor, one of the early promoters of white water safety & rescue programs. This is an excellent text, and provides a very good introduction to solo techniques.

Walbridge, C., & Sundmacher, W.A. (1995) *Whitewater Rescue Manual*, **Ragged Mountain Press, Camden, Maine**
Charlie Walbridge is the "Dean" of North American white water Safety, for many years he has been the Safety Chairman for the American Whitewater Affiliation. This is an up-to-date manual that should grace the shelf of every paddler who considers paddling on flowing water.

Internet "Web/WWW" Resources: (these do change quickly!)

Canadian Recreational Canoeing Association http://www.awa.org
- a good site that contains links to many paddling resources and other paddling groups.

Canadian Recreational Canoeing Association http://www.crca.ca
- one of the best Canadian starting places for Canadian paddling resources and groups.

Notes:

_____

_____

_____

_____

_____

_____

_____

_____

_____

_____

_____

_____

_____

_____

_____